# 106th Edition

## Travel to Birmingham Alabama

2023
People Who Know
Publishing
Jack Ross

Forward: In this book, People Who Know Publishing will provide a travel guide of 101+ things to see, do and visit in Birmingham Alabama. We strive to make our guides as comprehensive and complete as possible. We publish travel guides on cities and countries all over the world. Feel free to check out our complete list of travel guides here:

People Who Know Publishing partners with local experts to produce travel guides on various locations. We differentiate ourselves from other travel books by focusing on areas not typically covered by others. Our guides include a detailed history of the location and its population. In addition to covering all of the "must see" areas of a location such as museums and local sights, we also provide up-to-date restaurant suggestions and local food traditions.

To make a request for a travel guide on a particular area or to join our email list to stay updated on travel tips from local experts sign up here: https://mailchi.mp/c74b62620b1f/travel-books

Be sure to confirm restaurants, addresses, and phone numbers as those may have changed since the book was published.

About the Author:

Jack Ross is a college student who was born in Westchester County, NY. He's an expert on the local "in the know" tips of the area and is an authority on Westchester and its towns. He's been featured in several publications including Business Insider and CNBC for his books.

During his spare time, he writes, plays tennis and golf and enjoys all water sports (including his latest favorite, the eFoil). Jack also enjoys traveling and is a food connoisseur throughout Westchester. Jack travels consistently and has been to majority of the states in the U.S.

# Table of Contents

# Birmingham Alabama

*State:* Alabama

*Population:* 200,733

*Ranking in U.S.:* N/A

*County:* Jefferson County

*Founded:* 1871

*Tag line:* N/A

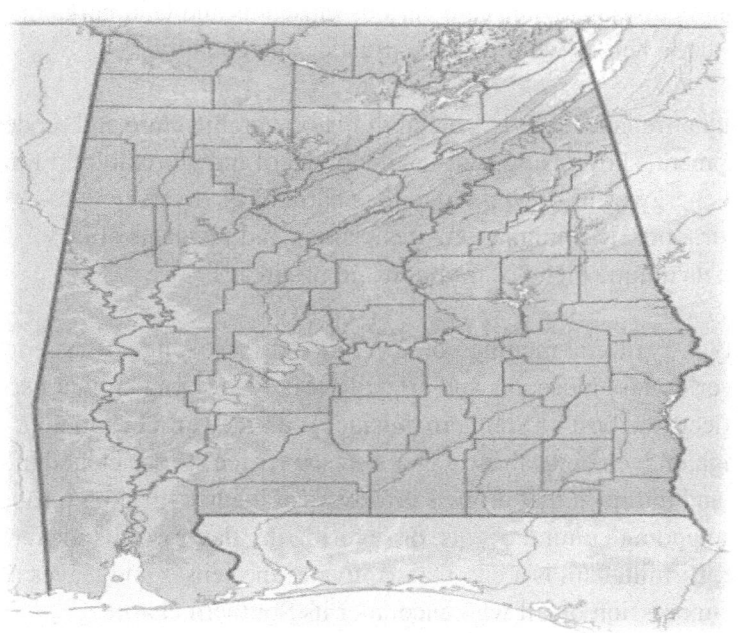

# Introduction

*"Birmingham is a city with a rich history and a vibrant culture, where the past and the present coexist." - Unknown*

Nestled in the heart of the southern United States, Birmingham, Alabama, stands as a city with a rich tapestry of history, culture, and resilience. Affectionately known as the "Magic City," Birmingham's story is deeply woven into the fabric of the American South. Originally established as an industrial hub in the late 19th century, Birmingham played a crucial role in the iron and steel industry, earning its nickname for the seemingly magical speed at which it grew.

Beyond its industrial roots, Birmingham holds a significant place in the narrative of the Civil Rights Movement. The city witnessed pivotal moments in the struggle for equality, with courageous individuals making history at places like the 16th Street Baptist Church. Today, the city honors this legacy through various museums and landmarks that pay tribute to the heroes who fought for justice and equality.

Birmingham's landscape is a blend of historic architecture and modern development, showcasing a city in the midst of transformation. From the vibrant energy of its downtown to the charm of its diverse neighborhoods, Birmingham invites visitors and residents alike to explore its unique blend of tradition and progress.

The city is a cultural melting pot, offering a diverse range of experiences, from world-class museums and art galleries to a thriving culinary scene that reflects the best of Southern cuisine. With its warm hospitality, Birmingham welcomes those eager to discover the stories etched into its streets and the spirit that propels it forward. Whether strolling through its parks, attending cultural events, or savoring the flavors of its local cuisine, Birmingham is a city that captivates the senses and leaves a lasting impression on all who encounter its Southern charm.

# History

Founding and Growth (1871): Birmingham was founded in 1871, emerging from the post-Civil War era. Its rapid growth was fueled by rich mineral resources, particularly iron ore, coal, and limestone.

Iron and Steel Industry: Birmingham became a major industrial center due to its proximity to these resources. The city earned its nickname, the "Magic City," for the seemingly overnight development of its iron and steel industry.

Industrial Expansion: By the early 20th century, Birmingham was a leading producer of iron and steel in the United States. Companies like U.S. Steel and Republic Steel had a significant presence, shaping the city's economic landscape.

Segregation and Civil Rights Struggles: Birmingham was a focal point of the Civil Rights Movement in the 1960s. The city was deeply segregated, and racial tensions were high.

Urban Renewal and Revitalization: In recent decades, Birmingham has undergone urban renewal and revitalization efforts. Historic districts have been preserved, and the city has diversified its economy, embracing healthcare, finance, and technology sectors.

Cultural Renaissance: Birmingham has experienced a cultural renaissance, with the development of cultural institutions, entertainment venues, and a burgeoning culinary scene. Regions Field, the Birmingham Museum of Art, and the Alabama Theatre contribute to the city's vibrant cultural landscape.

Birmingham's history is one of resilience, transformation, and a continual effort to overcome challenges. The city's evolution reflects broader trends in American history, from industrialization and racial struggles to economic shifts and urban revitalization. Today, Birmingham stands as a city that honors its past while embracing a future of diversity, progress, and cultural richness.

Deindustrialization: Like many Rust Belt cities, Birmingham faced economic challenges with the decline of heavy industry in the latter half of the 20th century. The steel industry, in particular, saw a significant downturn, leading to job losses and economic shifts.

# Economy

Economic Diversification:
Birmingham's economy has undergone significant diversification in recent decades, moving away from its historical reliance on heavy industry. While manufacturing, healthcare, and finance remain important sectors, the city has sought to broaden its economic base.

Key Economic Sectors:
Healthcare and Biotechnology: Birmingham has emerged as a major healthcare and biotechnology hub. The presence of the University of Alabama at Birmingham (UAB) and its medical center contributes significantly to this sector.

Finance and Banking: The financial services industry is another pillar of Birmingham's economy. The city hosts several regional and national banks, and it is considered a banking center for the region.

Technology and Innovation: Birmingham has made efforts to promote technology and innovation, with a focus on attracting startups and fostering entrepreneurship. Initiatives like Innovation Depot support the growth of tech-based businesses.

Education and Research: The presence of UAB, a leading research institution, has a substantial impact on Birmingham's economy. Research initiatives and collaborations contribute to the city's knowledge-based economy.

Manufacturing: While the steel industry has diminished, manufacturing remains a part of Birmingham's economic landscape. The city is involved in various manufacturing activities, including automotive production and aerospace.

Workforce and Employment:
Education and Workforce Development: Efforts have been made to align workforce development with the needs of the evolving economy, ensuring a skilled workforce for industries such as healthcare and technology.

Job Market: Birmingham's job market has seen growth in sectors like healthcare, finance, and professional services. The city has attracted a diverse range of employers contributing to its economic vitality.

# Transportation Systems

Roads and Highways:
Interstate Highways: Birmingham is a major transportation hub with several interstate highways converging in the area. These include I-20, I-65, and I-59, facilitating regional and national connectivity.

Local Roads: The city has an extensive network of local roads and streets. Downtown Birmingham is characterized by a grid system, making it relatively easy to navigate.

Public Transit:
MAX Transit: The Birmingham-Jefferson County Transit Authority operates the MAX Transit system, providing bus services throughout the city and surrounding areas. MAX Transit offers various routes to connect residents with key destinations.

Rail Transportation:
Rail Service: Birmingham has a history deeply tied to railroads, and rail transportation remains an important part of the city's logistics and industrial infrastructure. The city is served by both freight and passenger rail services.

Airports:
Birmingham-Shuttlesworth International Airport: This airport serves the greater Birmingham area and provides domestic and limited international flights. It is located approximately 5 miles northeast of downtown Birmingham.

Biking and Walking:
Bike-Friendly Initiatives: Birmingham has been working on becoming more bike-friendly, with the development of bike lanes and initiatives to encourage cycling. The city has also seen efforts to improve pedestrian infrastructure, making it more walkable in certain areas.

Future Developments:
Transportation Planning: Like many growing cities, Birmingham is engaged in ongoing transportation planning to address current and future needs. This includes considerations for infrastructure improvements, public transit expansion, and overall mobility.

.

# Neighborhoods

*Downtown Birmingham:*
*Description: The heart of the city, Downtown Birmingham is a mix of historic and modern buildings. It's home to government buildings, businesses, entertainment venues, and cultural institutions.*
*Key Features: The area includes the historic Five Points South district, the financial district, and attractions like Railroad Park.*

*Southside:*
*Description: Southside is a dynamic and eclectic area known for its diverse population, historic homes, and cultural amenities. It's home to the University of Alabama at Birmingham (UAB).*
*Key Features: Five Points South, with its restaurants, bars, and entertainment venues, is a central hub. The neighborhood also includes the UAB campus.*

*Highland Park:*
*Description: Highland Park is characterized by tree-lined streets and historic architecture. It's a residential neighborhood with a mix of single-family homes and apartments.*
*Key Features: Highland Park is known for its parks, such as Rushton Park, and the historic Highland Park Golf Course.*

*Forest Park:*
*Description: Forest Park is an affluent residential neighborhood with a mix of architectural styles. It features tree-lined streets, parks, and a sense of community.*
*Key Features: Forest Park is known for its historic Avondale Park, upscale homes, and the popular Avondale commercial district with breweries and restaurants.*

# Food

*Barbecue:*
*Description: Birmingham is known for its delicious barbecue, with a variety of styles and flavors. From pulled pork to smoked chicken, you can find mouthwatering barbecue joints throughout the city.*
*Recommendation: Try some ribs or pulled pork from local favorites like Saw's BBQ or Miss Myra's Pit Bar-B-Q.*

*Soul Food:*
*Description: Soul food is a staple in Birmingham, reflecting the city's cultural heritage. Expect comfort food like fried chicken, collard greens, cornbread, and macaroni and cheese.*
*Recommendation: Check out Niki's West for a classic meat-and-three experience, serving Southern comfort food.*

*Biscuits and Gravy:*
*Description: A Southern breakfast classic, biscuits and gravy are a popular morning dish in Birmingham. Fluffy biscuits smothered in creamy sausage gravy make for a hearty start to the day.*
*Recommendation: Visit Over Easy in Mountain Brook for a delicious breakfast featuring biscuits and gravy.*

*Hot Chicken:*
*Description: Nashville's hot chicken trend has made its way to Birmingham. Expect crispy, spicy fried chicken served with pickles and often accompanied by cooling sides like coleslaw.*
*Recommendation: Check out Eugene's Hot Chicken for a tasty and fiery hot chicken experience.*

*Pimento Cheese:*
*Description: Pimento cheese is a Southern favorite, made with sharp cheddar cheese, mayonnaise, and diced pimentos. It's often used as a spread on sandwiches or as a dip.*
*Recommendation: Visit The Pizitz Food Hall, where you can find vendors serving creative dishes featuring pimento cheese.*

# Here are our ten favorite restaurant recommendations!

*1.A James Beard Award-winning restaurant, Highlands Bar and Grill, led by Chef Frank Stitt, is celebrated for its sophisticated Southern cuisine and commitment to using locally sourced ingredients.*

*2.Another culinary gem from Chef Frank Stitt, Bottega offers a menu inspired by the flavors of Italy. The restaurant is known for its elegant atmosphere and creative, seasonal dishes.*

*3.Helmed by Chef Chris Hastings, Hot and Hot Fish Club is renowned for its innovative Southern cuisine. The menu features locally sourced, seasonal ingredients prepared with a modern twist.*

*4.Sister restaurant to Highlands Bar and Grill, Chez Fonfon offers a cozy bistro atmosphere with a menu influenced by French cuisine. The restaurant is known for its classic dishes and casual ambiance.*

*5.El Barrio is a popular spot for Mexican cuisine with a modern twist. Known for its vibrant atmosphere, the restaurant serves tacos, creative cocktails, and a variety of Mexican-inspired dishes.*

*6.Saw's Soul Kitchen is a local favorite for barbecue and Southern comfort food. The menu includes pulled pork, ribs, and classic sides, served in a laid-back, casual setting.*

7.Fero, located in Pizitz Food Hall, offers modern Italian cuisine with a focus on fresh, high-quality ingredients. The menu includes handmade pasta, wood-fired pizzas, and more.

8.Chef Chris Hastings' OvenBird is known for its wood-fired cooking and Latin-inspired flavors. The menu features a variety of small plates, grilled meats, and inventive dishes.

9.Roots and Revelry, located in the historic Thomas Jefferson Tower, offers an eclectic menu with American and international influences. The restaurant has a stylish, contemporary atmosphere.

10.Ashley Mac's is a local favorite for comfort food and Southern-inspired dishes. Known for its delicious cakes and casseroles, the restaurant offers a range of options for dine-in or takeout.

# Nightlife

*The Collins Bar is known for its expertly crafted cocktails and sophisticated atmosphere. The bartenders are skilled mixologists, and the bar offers a stylish setting for a night out.*

*The Atomic Lounge is a quirky and retro-inspired cocktail lounge with a vibrant atmosphere. It's a favorite spot for creative drinks, live music, and a unique, eclectic decor.*

*Located in downtown Birmingham, The Wine Loft offers an extensive selection of wines and a chic atmosphere. It's a great place for wine enthusiasts and those looking for a more relaxed setting.*

*Tucked away behind a hidden door, Paper Doll Bar exudes a speakeasy vibe with its craft cocktails and intimate setting. It's a popular spot for those seeking a more clandestine atmosphere.*

*Iron City is a versatile venue that hosts live music performances, comedy shows, and other events. It's a great place to catch a concert and enjoy a night out with friends.*

*Carrigan's is a popular spot for its extensive beer selection, creative cocktails, and gastropub fare. The atmosphere is casual and inviting, making it a favorite for locals.*

*Brennan's Irish Pub offers a genuine Irish pub experience with a selection of Irish and local beers, hearty pub food, and live music. It's a lively spot for a friendly and relaxed atmosphere.*

# Local Traditions & Customs

*Southern Hospitality:*

*Description: Birmingham, like much of the South, is known for its tradition of Southern hospitality. This includes a warm and welcoming demeanor, politeness, and a willingness to help others.*

*Culinary Traditions:*

*Description: Southern cuisine plays a significant role in local traditions. Barbecue, fried chicken, biscuits, and other comfort foods are often enjoyed at family gatherings, community events, and local celebrations.*

*Church and Faith:*

*Description: The South, including Birmingham, has a strong religious tradition. Church attendance is a common custom, and faith often plays a central role in community life. Religious events and celebrations are integral to the local culture.*

*Music and Arts:*

*Description: Birmingham has a vibrant music and arts scene that reflects the cultural diversity of the city. Local traditions include music festivals, art exhibits, and events that celebrate the contributions of artists to the community.*

*Football and Sports Culture:*

*Description: Sports, particularly football, are deeply ingrained in the local culture. Supporting local college teams like the University of Alabama at Birmingham (UAB) Blazers or the Alabama Crimson Tide is a significant tradition for many residents.*

# What to buy?

*Iron and Steel Artwork:*

*Birmingham's history is closely tied to the iron and steel industry. Look for locally crafted iron and steel artwork, sculptures, or decorative items that pay homage to the city's industrial heritage.*

*Craft Beer and Spirits:*

*Birmingham has a growing craft beer and spirits scene. Consider purchasing locally brewed beers, spirits, or merchandise from one of the city's breweries or distilleries.*

*Peanut Brittle:*

*Alabama is known for its delicious peanut brittle. You can find locally made versions at specialty shops or markets throughout Birmingham. It makes for a sweet and crunchy souvenir.*

*Local Art and Crafts:*

*Explore the city's art galleries and markets for unique pieces created by local artists. This could include paintings, ceramics, jewelry, or other handmade crafts that capture the spirit of Birmingham.*

*Barbecue Sauces and Rubs:*

*Birmingham takes its barbecue seriously, and you can find a variety of locally produced barbecue sauces and rubs. Look for products from popular barbecue joints or specialty stores.*

# Finally, here are the five most famous people from the city!

*1.Angela Davis:*
*Occupation: Political Activist, Author, Scholar*
*Description: Angela Davis, born in Birmingham, is a prominent political activist and scholar known for her involvement in the Civil Rights Movement and her advocacy for prison abolition. She is also a distinguished author and professor.*

*2.Condoleezza Rice:*
*Occupation: Diplomat, Political Scientist*
*Description: Condoleezza Rice, born in Birmingham, served as the 66th United States Secretary of State under President George W. Bush. Prior to her political career, she was a political science professor and is currently a professor at Stanford University.*

*3.Ruben Studdard:*
*Occupation: Singer, Musician*
*Description: Ruben Studdard, also known as the "Velvet Teddy Bear," gained fame as the winner of the second season of "American Idol." The R&B and gospel singer was born and raised in Birmingham.*

*4.Hank Aaron:*
*Occupation: Baseball Player*
*Description: Hank Aaron, widely regarded as one of baseball's greatest players, was born in Mobile, Alabama, but later lived in and had connections to Birmingham. He broke Babe Ruth's home run record and was a trailblazer in the sport.*

*5.Nell Carter:*
*Occupation: Actress, Singer*
*Description: Nell Carter, an accomplished actress and singer, was born in Birmingham. She is best known for her role in the television series "Gimme a Break!" and her work on Broadway, where she won a Tony Award for her performance in "Ain't Misbehavin'."*

# 101+ things to do in the city

1. Visit the Birmingham Civil Rights Institute.
2. Walk through Kelly Ingram Park.
3. Explore the 16th Street Baptist Church.
4. Attend a performance at the Alabama Theatre.
5. Hike the trails at Ruffner Mountain.
6. Stroll around Railroad Park.
7. Tour the Sloss Furnaces National Historic Landmark.
8. Visit the Birmingham Museum of Art.
9. Attend a concert at Iron City Birmingham.
10. Explore the Birmingham Botanical Gardens.
11. Take a scenic drive on the Red Mountain Expressway.
12. Attend a Birmingham Barons baseball game.
13. Enjoy a show at the Lyric Theatre.
14. Visit Vulcan Park and Museum.
15. Explore the McWane Science Center.
16. Attend the Sidewalk Film Festival.
17. Visit the Negro Southern League Museum.
18. Check out the murals in the Avondale neighborhood.
19. Have a picnic at Linn Park.
20. Explore the Birmingham Zoo.
21. Take a historic walking tour of the city.
22. Attend the Moss Rock Festival.
23. Walk along the Rotary Trail.
24. Visit the Southern Museum of Flight.
25. Explore the Five Points South Historic District.
26. Attend a UAB Blazers basketball game.
27. Take a brewery tour in the Avondale Brewing District.
28. Experience the Birmingham Ghost Walk.
29. Attend the Birmingham Greek Festival.
30. Explore the Pepper Place Saturday Market.
31. Take a bike ride along the Jones Valley Trail.
32. Attend a performance at the Alys Stephens Performing Arts Center.
33. Explore the Historic Rickwood Field.
34. Attend the Magic City Art Connection.
35. Visit the Birmingham Civil Rights National Monument.
36. Explore the Birmingham Negro Southern League Baseball Museum.
37. Attend the Birmingham Art Crawl.
38. Go zip-lining at Red Mountain Park.
39. Visit the Arlington Antebellum Home and Gardens.
40. Take a food tour in the city.

41. Attend a Birmingham Bulls hockey game.
42. Explore the Birmingham Oddities and Curiosities Market.
43. Attend the Fiesta Birmingham Latino Festival.
44. Take a paddleboat ride at Railroad Park.
45. Attend the Alabama Ballet performance.
46. Explore the Birmingham Fire Museum.
47. Take a scenic drive along the Shades Crest Road.
48. Attend the Taste of 4th Avenue Jazz Festival.
49. Explore the Birmingham Food Truck Roundup.
50. Attend the Do Dah Day Parade.
51. Take a historic tour of the Arlington House.
52. Attend the Birmingham International Street Fair.
53. Explore the Birmingham Historic Touring Company.
54. Attend the Greater Birmingham Humane Society's Jazz Cat Ball.
55. Take a cooking class in the city.
56. Explore the Freedom Walk at Kelly Ingram Park.
57. Attend the Alabama Asian Cultures and Food Festival.
58. Take a self-guided mural tour in Woodlawn.
59. Visit the Oak Hill Cemetery.
60. Attend a play at the Virginia Samford Theatre.
61. Explore the Village Creek Greenway.
62. Attend the Birmingham Ethnic Festival.
63. Take a scenic drive on Highway 280.
64. Explore the Ensley SoHo neighborhood.
65. Attend a film screening at the Birmingham Public Library.
66. Take a yoga class at Railroad Park.
67. Attend the Alabama Multicultural Street Fair.
68. Explore the Birmingham Black Barons Hall of Fame.
69. Take a day trip to Oak Mountain State Park.
70. Attend the Birmingham Record Fair.
71. Explore the Birmingham Mural Trail.
72. Attend the Birmingham Restaurant Week.
73. Take a hike at Moss Rock Preserve.
74. Attend the Birmingham Fashion Week.
75. Explore the Liberty Park Sports Complex.
76. Attend the Funky Fish Fry at the Birmingham Zoo.
77. Take a stroll through the Birmingham Farmers Market.
78. Attend a performance by the Alabama Symphony Orchestra.
79. Explore the 20th Street North Historic District.
80. Attend the Birmingham Hammerfest.
81. Take a pottery class at Red Dot Gallery.

82.Explore the Birmingham Originals Restaurant Week.
83.Attend a Birmingham Children's Theatre production.
84.Take a scenic drive along Cahaba Beach Road.
85.Attend the Birmingham Arts and Music Festival.
86.Explore the Historic Fountain Heights neighborhood.
87.Attend the Do It Downtown Festival.
88.Take a horseback riding tour at Griffin Farms.
89.Attend the Birmingham Air Show.
90. Explore the historic Glen Iris Park neighborhood.
91.Attend the Birmingham Carnival.
92.Take a historic tour of the Boyles House.
93.Attend the Market at Pepper Place.
94.Explore the historic Bethel Baptist Church.
95.Attend the Birmingham Boat Show.
96.Take a hot air balloon ride over the city.
97.Attend the Birmingham RV Super Show.
98.Explore the Cahaba River National Wildlife Refuge.
99.Attend the Birmingham Military Tattoo.
100.Take a pottery class at MakeBHM.
101.Attend the Birmingham Multicultural Festival.
102.Explore the Vulcan Trail.
103.Attend the Birmingham Big Art Show.
104.Take a scenic drive along Mount Laurel.
105.Attend a performance at the Terrific New Theatre.
106.Explore the Arlington-West End neighborhood.
107.Attend the Birmingham Music Festival.
108.Take a day trip to the American Village in Montevallo.
109.Explore the Brown-Marx Building.
110.Attend the Barber Vintage Festival.

# 1. Visit the Birmingham Civil Rights Institute.

A visit to the Birmingham Civil Rights Institute is an immersive and deeply moving experience that takes you on a profound journey through a crucial chapter in American history. Located in downtown Birmingham, this museum stands as a poignant tribute to the struggle for civil rights during the pivotal years of the 1950s and 1960s. The exhibits within the institute are meticulously curated, featuring a compelling mix of artifacts, photographs, documents, and multimedia presentations that vividly portray the challenges faced and the triumphs achieved by those who fought for justice and equality.

As you walk through the museum, you'll encounter powerful narratives that highlight the resilience of individuals who played key roles in the Civil Rights Movement. The oral histories shared within the exhibits provide firsthand accounts, offering a personal and emotional connection to the events that unfolded in Birmingham and the broader fight against racial injustice.

One of the museum's notable features is its focus on Birmingham's unique place in history, particularly with the infamous 16th Street Baptist Church bombing and the subsequent marches that took place in the city. The institute is situated near Kelly Ingram Park, where you can extend your exploration to witness captivating sculptures and monuments that serve as a visceral reminder of the struggles faced by activists.

Beyond the historical significance, the Birmingham Civil Rights Institute serves as a platform for reflection and education. It encourages visitors to consider the ongoing quest for civil rights, fostering a dialogue about the importance of equality and justice in contemporary society. The institute's commitment to preserving and sharing this crucial history contributes to the city's identity and serves as a testament to the resilience of those who fought for a more just and equitable future.

In summary, a visit to the Birmingham Civil Rights Institute is a transformative experience, offering not only a comprehensive understanding of the past but also an opportunity for reflection and contemplation on the continued journey toward a more inclusive and equal society.

# 2.Walk through Kelly Ingram Park.

Walking through Kelly Ingram Park is a poignant and reflective experience, offering a serene yet powerful setting that serves as both a memorial and an outdoor gallery commemorating the struggles and triumphs of the Civil Rights Movement. Situated adjacent to the Birmingham Civil Rights Institute, the park is a significant historical landmark in downtown Birmingham.

As you stroll through Kelly Ingram Park, you'll encounter a series of striking sculptures, monuments, and installations that vividly capture the spirit of the Civil Rights Movement. The most notable among them is the powerful "Four Spirits" sculpture, dedicated to the four young girls—Addie Mae Collins, Cynthia Wesley, Carole Robertson, and Denise McNair—who lost their lives in the 16th Street Baptist Church bombing in 1963. The memorial is a solemn and moving tribute, reminding visitors of the sacrifices made during this tumultuous period in history.

The park's design incorporates elements that invite contemplation, such as the "Freedom Walk" pathway, lined with inscriptions and quotes that provide context and insight into the events that unfolded in Birmingham. The strategically placed sculptures, like those depicting police dogs and water cannons, recreate the scenes of nonviolent protests and bring the past to life.

Kelly Ingram Park is not only a space for reflection but also a place for education and remembrance. The combination of artistic expression and historical significance makes it a must-visit destination for anyone interested in gaining a deeper understanding of the Civil Rights Movement. The park's location adjacent to the Birmingham Civil Rights Institute creates a seamless and complementary experience, allowing visitors to seamlessly transition between indoor and outdoor exhibits, creating a comprehensive and emotionally impactful exploration of this critical chapter in American history.

# 3.Explore the 16th Street Baptist Church.

Exploring the 16th Street Baptist Church is a profound and historically significant experience, as this iconic church played a pivotal role in the Civil Rights Movement. Located in downtown Birmingham, Alabama, the church stands as both a place of worship and a symbol of resilience in the face of racial injustice.

The 16th Street Baptist Church gained international attention when, on September 15, 1963, a tragic bombing claimed the lives of four African American girls: Addie Mae Collins, Cynthia Wesley, Carole Robertson, and Denise McNair. The bombing was a heinous act of racial violence during a tumultuous period in the struggle for civil rights.

Upon entering the church, visitors are greeted by the historic sanctuary, which has been meticulously preserved. The stained glass windows and interior reflect the church's role as a spiritual and communal center for Birmingham's African American community. The basement, where the explosion occurred, serves as a poignant memorial, reminding visitors of the lives lost and the ongoing fight for justice.

The 16th Street Baptist Church is not only a site of historical significance but also a living testament to the resilience of the Birmingham community. Over the years, the church has become a symbol of the Civil Rights Movement's sacrifices and a beacon for those advocating for equality.

In addition to its historical importance, the church remains an active place of worship. Attending a service or event allows visitors to experience the vibrant community that continues to thrive within its walls.

Exploring the 16th Street Baptist Church provides a tangible connection to the struggles and triumphs of the Civil Rights Movement. The church's commitment to preserving its history and promoting social justice makes it a must-visit destination for those seeking a deeper understanding of the ongoing journey toward equality and justice in the United States.

# 4.Attend a performance at the Alabama Theatre.

Attending a performance at the Alabama Theatre is a delightful and culturally enriching experience. Located in the heart of downtown Birmingham, this historic venue is a true gem with its stunning architecture and rich history. Built in 1927, the Alabama Theatre is a Spanish-Moorish style movie palace that has been lovingly preserved and restored, making it a unique and atmospheric setting for various performances.

Whether you're attending a live concert, a Broadway show, a classic film screening, or any other event hosted at the theatre, you're in for a treat. The grandeur of the interior, characterized by ornate detailing, a starlit sky ceiling, and a beautifully restored Wurlitzer organ, creates an immersive and nostalgic ambiance that transports you to a bygone era.

The Alabama Theatre has hosted a wide range of performances, from musical acts and theatrical productions to comedy shows and film festivals. Its versatility and charm make it a beloved cultural institution in Birmingham, attracting both locals and visitors seeking top-notch entertainment in a historic setting.

Before or after the performance, take some time to appreciate the surrounding area. The theatre is situated in the vibrant downtown district, offering opportunities to explore nearby restaurants, cafes, and other attractions. Whether you attend a performance for the nostalgia, the artistic excellence, or the sheer enjoyment of live entertainment, the Alabama Theatre provides an unforgettable and enriching experience for patrons of all ages.

# 5.Hike the trails at Ruffner Mountain.

Hiking the trails at Ruffner Mountain Nature Preserve is a rejuvenating and immersive outdoor experience. Located just a short drive from downtown Birmingham, Ruffner Mountain offers a diverse network of trails that cater to various skill levels, providing hikers with a chance to explore the natural beauty of the area.

As you embark on the trails, you'll encounter a mix of wooded paths, scenic overlooks, and meandering streams, creating a picturesque setting for your hike. The trail system is well-maintained, offering options for both casual strolls and more challenging hikes for those seeking a bit of adventure.

One of the highlights of Ruffner Mountain is the peacefulness and tranquility it provides, allowing hikers to escape the hustle and bustle of the city and immerse themselves in the beauty of nature. The nature preserve is home to a variety of flora and fauna, and birdwatchers will appreciate the diverse bird species that inhabit the area.

For a panoramic view of Birmingham and its surrounding landscape, make your way to Hawk's View Overlook. The breathtaking scenery from this vantage point is a rewarding treat for those who reach the summit.

Ruffner Mountain Nature Preserve is not just a hiking destination; it's also a hub for environmental education and conservation efforts. Take the time to visit the Nature Center to learn more about the local ecology, wildlife, and ongoing conservation initiatives.

Whether you're a seasoned hiker or a nature enthusiast looking for a peaceful escape, hiking the trails at Ruffner Mountain provides a wonderful opportunity to connect with the outdoors, breathe in the fresh air, and appreciate the natural beauty that surrounds Birmingham. It's a perfect way to spend a day in nature, enjoying the serenity and scenic landscapes that Ruffner Mountain has to offer.

# 6.Stroll around Railroad Park.

Taking a leisurely stroll around Railroad Park is a delightful and refreshing experience. Situated in the heart of downtown Birmingham, this urban green space offers a perfect blend of relaxation, recreation, and community engagement. Whether you're looking for a peaceful escape, a spot for outdoor activities, or a vibrant gathering place, Railroad Park has something for everyone.

As you explore the park, you'll encounter beautifully landscaped areas, scenic walking paths, and charming water features. The picturesque lake and streams add a serene ambiance, creating a peaceful retreat amidst the urban landscape. The park's thoughtful design incorporates native plants and greenery, providing a welcome respite from the hustle and bustle of city life.

Railroad Park is more than just a place to stroll; it's a hub of community activity. You may come across locals enjoying picnics, families playing in the designated play areas, or fitness enthusiasts engaging in outdoor workouts. The park often hosts events, festivals, and live performances, contributing to its lively and inclusive atmosphere.

For those interested in fitness, the park features a well-maintained walking and jogging trail, providing a scenic route for exercise. Additionally, the park is equipped with exercise stations, making it a popular destination for those seeking an outdoor workout.

The park's central location makes it an ideal starting or stopping point for exploring other downtown attractions, restaurants, and cultural venues. The proximity to the Railroad Park Foundation and Regions Field, home of the Birmingham Barons baseball team, adds to the overall vibrancy of the area.

Whether you're seeking solitude, enjoying a leisurely walk, or participating in community events, a stroll around Railroad Park offers a dynamic and inviting experience. It's a testament to Birmingham's commitment to creating accessible green spaces that enhance the quality of life for residents and visitors alike.

# 7. Tour the Sloss Furnaces National Historic Landmark.

Touring the Sloss Furnaces National Historic Landmark is a fascinating and immersive journey into Birmingham's industrial past. Located just a short drive from downtown, Sloss Furnaces stands as a testament to the city's role in the iron and steel industry during the late 19th and early 20th centuries.

As you explore the site, you'll discover a well-preserved industrial complex that once played a crucial role in Birmingham's rise as an industrial powerhouse. The towering blast furnaces, intricate machinery, and industrial structures provide a tangible glimpse into the city's industrial heritage. The landmark is particularly renowned for its unique design, featuring blast furnaces that resemble towering sentinels against the skyline.

Guided tours of Sloss Furnaces offer insights into the iron-making process, the working conditions of the laborers, and the historical significance of the site. You'll learn about the challenges and triumphs of Birmingham's industrial evolution, from the early days of iron production to the site's later use as a creative space for artists.

Sloss Furnaces also serves as a cultural center, hosting events, art installations, and educational programs. The Sloss Metal Arts Program, for example, provides artists with studio space to create unique works inspired by the industrial surroundings.

One of the most iconic features of Sloss Furnaces is the annual "Fright Furnace" event, where the historic site is transformed into a haunted attraction during the Halloween season. It's a creative way to experience the site in a different light while still appreciating its historical significance.

The National Historic Landmark designation recognizes Sloss Furnaces as a crucial piece of American industrial history, and visiting the site allows you to connect with Birmingham's past in a tangible and immersive way. Whether you're a history enthusiast, an art lover, or simply curious about the city's industrial roots, a tour of Sloss Furnaces provides a captivating and educational experience.

# 8.Visit the Birmingham Museum of Art.

Visiting the Birmingham Museum of Art (BMA) promises an enriching and culturally immersive experience. Situated in the heart of downtown Birmingham, this museum is a vibrant hub for art enthusiasts and curious visitors alike. The BMA boasts an extensive and diverse collection that spans centuries and encompasses various art forms, making it a must-visit destination for those seeking a deeper understanding of artistic expression.

As you explore the museum's galleries, you'll encounter an impressive array of artwork, including paintings, sculptures, decorative arts, and more. The collection features both classical and contemporary pieces, showcasing a wide range of styles and artistic movements. Notable artists from different periods are represented, providing a comprehensive overview of art history.

The museum's commitment to community engagement is evident through its educational programs, special exhibitions, and events. These initiatives aim to make art accessible and enjoyable for visitors of all ages. The museum often hosts lectures, workshops, and interactive activities that enhance the overall visitor experience.

One of the highlights of the Birmingham Museum of Art is its Asian art collection, which is considered one of the most comprehensive in the Southeast. The collection includes exquisite pieces from China, Japan, Korea, and South Asia, offering a unique opportunity to explore the rich cultural heritage of these regions.

The BMA's dedication to showcasing local artists is evident in its contemporary art exhibitions, providing a platform for emerging talents within the Birmingham art scene. The museum's rotating exhibits ensure that each visit offers a fresh and dynamic perspective on the world of art.

The museum building itself is an architectural gem, featuring a modern design that complements the art within its walls. The spacious and well-lit galleries create an inviting atmosphere for contemplation and appreciation.

Whether you're a seasoned art enthusiast or a casual visitor, the Birmingham Museum of Art provides a captivating and thought-provoking experience. It serves as a cultural anchor for the community, fostering a love for the arts and contributing to Birmingham's vibrant cultural landscape.

# 9.Attend a concert at Iron City Birmingham.

Attending a concert at Iron City Birmingham is an electrifying and immersive experience that combines the thrill of live music with the unique ambiance of this historic venue. Located in the heart of downtown Birmingham, Iron City has established itself as a premier concert and event space, offering a dynamic setting for music enthusiasts.

As you step into Iron City, you'll be greeted by its industrial-chic atmosphere, featuring exposed brick walls and a spacious layout that creates an intimate connection between the performers and the audience. The venue's commitment to providing a top-notch audio and visual experience enhances the overall enjoyment of the concert.

Iron City hosts a diverse range of musical acts, from emerging artists to well-established bands across various genres. Whether you're into rock, indie, country, or electronic music, the venue's eclectic lineup ensures there's something for everyone. The intimate setting allows for an up-close and personal connection with the artists, making each performance a memorable and immersive experience.

The venue's versatility is not limited to concerts alone; it also serves as a space for special events, private parties, and community gatherings. The rooftop garden offers a unique outdoor space with panoramic views of the city skyline, providing an additional dimension to the Iron City experience.

Before or after the concert, you can explore the surrounding area, taking advantage of the vibrant downtown scene. Whether it's grabbing a bite to eat at one of the nearby restaurants, exploring other entertainment options, or simply enjoying the city lights, Iron City's central location allows for a seamless integration into Birmingham's nightlife.

Attending a concert at Iron City Birmingham is more than just a musical event; it's a cultural and social experience that contributes to the city's dynamic and evolving arts scene. The venue's commitment to providing an exceptional live music experience makes it a standout destination for both locals and visitors looking to enjoy the best of Birmingham's musical offerings.

# 10.Explore the Birmingham Botanical Gardens.

Exploring the Birmingham Botanical Gardens is a serene and visually stunning experience that allows you to connect with nature in the heart of the city. Situated just a short drive from downtown Birmingham, this expansive botanical oasis offers a diverse array of gardens, plant collections, and educational spaces, making it a beloved destination for botany enthusiasts and casual visitors alike.

As you wander through the Birmingham Botanical Gardens, you'll discover themed gardens that showcase a wide variety of plant species, from vibrant flowers to lush greenery. The Gardens feature specialized areas such as the Japanese Gardens, Rose Gardens, and Southern Living Gardens, each providing a unique and aesthetically pleasing environment.

One of the highlights is the impressive Kaul Wildflower Garden, which showcases native plants in their natural habitats. This garden not only offers a beautiful display but also serves as an educational resource for conservation and sustainable landscaping practices.

The Dunn Formal Rose Garden is another enchanting spot, boasting a breathtaking array of roses in various colors and varieties. It's a perfect place for a leisurely stroll or to simply bask in the beauty of blooming flowers.

The Birmingham Botanical Gardens also houses the Hill Garden, a tranquil space featuring a large reflecting pool surrounded by seasonal plantings. This area provides a peaceful retreat for contemplation and relaxation.

For those interested in educational experiences, the Gardens host workshops, classes, and events that cater to all ages. The Leaf & Petal Café offers a delightful place to grab a bite, and the gift shop provides an opportunity to take home a botanical-inspired souvenir.

Beyond its role as a recreational space, the Birmingham Botanical Gardens plays a crucial role in conservation and environmental education. Its commitment to sustainability and the preservation of plant species contributes to the overall well-being of the community.

Whether you're an avid botanist, a nature lover, or someone looking for a tranquil escape, the Birmingham Botanical Gardens provides a captivating and rejuvenating experience. It's a haven of natural beauty that adds to the cultural richness of Birmingham and serves as a testament to the importance of preserving and celebrating plant life.

# 11. Take a scenic drive on the Red Mountain Expressway.

Taking a scenic drive on the Red Mountain Expressway offers a breathtaking journey through the heart of Birmingham, showcasing panoramic views of the city's skyline and the surrounding landscape. This iconic expressway, also known as US-31/US-280, winds its way along the ridge of Red Mountain, providing drivers with spectacular vistas and glimpses of Birmingham's diverse neighborhoods.

Beginning the drive, you'll appreciate the elevated vantage point that Red Mountain Expressway offers, allowing you to see the city unfold before you. The skyline, characterized by a mix of modern and historic buildings, creates a striking visual contrast against the natural backdrop.

As you traverse the expressway, you'll encounter stunning overlooks that provide unobstructed views of downtown Birmingham, the vibrant UAB campus, and the surrounding hills. The scenic beauty is particularly captivating during sunrise or sunset when the warm hues of the sky complement the city lights and the natural landscape.

Red Mountain Expressway not only offers visual delights but also serves as a convenient route for exploring various neighborhoods and attractions in Birmingham. The drive takes you through areas such as Homewood, offering opportunities to explore local shops, restaurants, and parks along the way.

For those interested in history, the drive provides glimpses of iconic landmarks like Vulcan Park and Museum, where the towering Vulcan statue stands as a symbol of Birmingham's industrial heritage. The expressway also passes by Sloss Furnaces, contributing to the historical tapestry of the city.

Whether you're a local seeking a scenic route for a leisurely drive or a visitor eager to capture the essence of Birmingham from a unique perspective, the Red Mountain Expressway offers an unforgettable experience. It's a route that not only connects different parts of the city but also allows you to appreciate the diverse and dynamic character of Birmingham against the backdrop of its natural beauty.

# 12.Attend a Birmingham Barons baseball game.

Attending a Birmingham Barons baseball game is a quintessential American pastime and a thrilling experience for sports enthusiasts. The Barons, the Double-A affiliate of the Chicago White Sox, play their home games at Regions Field, located in the heart of downtown Birmingham.

The atmosphere at a Birmingham Barons game is energetic and family-friendly, providing an opportunity to enjoy America's favorite pastime in a vibrant setting. Regions Field, with its modern amenities and scenic views of the city skyline, enhances the overall enjoyment of the baseball experience.

Before the game, you can explore the ballpark, taking in the sights and sounds of the pre-game festivities. Regions Field offers a variety of seating options, from traditional grandstand seats to unique vantage points like the outfield lawn and the party suites, allowing fans to tailor their experience to their preferences.

The Birmingham Barons' games are not just about the action on the field; they also feature entertaining between-inning activities, promotions, and opportunities to engage with the community. Whether it's catching a foul ball, participating in the seventh-inning stretch, or enjoying the camaraderie of fellow fans, the entire experience contributes to the joy of attending a live baseball game.

Regions Field is equipped with amenities like concessions offering classic ballpark fare, making it easy to indulge in hot dogs, peanuts, and other favorite snacks. The open and friendly atmosphere creates a sense of community, making the game a social event as much as a sporting one.

Attending a Birmingham Barons baseball game allows you to connect with the city's sports culture, support local talent, and enjoy a classic American pastime in a modern and welcoming setting. Whether you're a dedicated baseball fan or someone looking for a fun and lively outing, a visit to Regions Field for a Birmingham Barons game is sure to be a home run.

# 13.Enjoy a show at the Lyric Theatre.

Enjoying a show at the Lyric Theatre is a captivating and culturally enriching experience. Located in the heart of downtown Birmingham, the Lyric Theatre stands as a historic landmark and a vibrant venue for live performances, ranging from concerts and musicals to comedy shows and theatrical productions.

Built in 1914, the Lyric Theatre has undergone extensive restoration to preserve its original grandeur while incorporating modern amenities. The architectural beauty, characterized by ornate detailing and a majestic stage, creates an intimate and elegant atmosphere that enhances the overall enjoyment of the performance.

Attending a show at the Lyric Theatre allows you to immerse yourself in the arts and entertainment scene of Birmingham. The venue hosts a diverse array of events, catering to a wide range of tastes and preferences. Whether you're a fan of classic Broadway productions, contemporary musical acts, or stand-up comedy, the Lyric Theatre's eclectic lineup ensures there's something for everyone.

The acoustics and visual design of the theater contribute to an exceptional viewing and listening experience. The carefully curated performances and the historic ambiance make each visit to the Lyric Theatre a memorable and special occasion.

Before or after the show, you can explore the surrounding area, taking advantage of the vibrant downtown scene. Whether it's grabbing a meal at one of the nearby restaurants, enjoying a drink at a local bar, or simply strolling through the city streets, the Lyric Theatre's central location allows for a seamless integration into Birmingham's cultural and social offerings.

Attending a show at the Lyric Theatre is more than just a form of entertainment; it's a celebration of the arts and a connection to Birmingham's rich cultural heritage. The venue's commitment to preserving its historic charm while embracing contemporary performances makes it a cherished destination for both locals and visitors seeking a unique and memorable entertainment experience.

# 14. Visit Vulcan Park and Museum.

Visiting Vulcan Park and Museum is a captivating and educational experience that offers a panoramic view of Birmingham and provides insights into the city's industrial history. Situated atop Red Mountain, this iconic landmark is home to the Vulcan statue, the world's largest cast iron statue and a symbol of Birmingham's industrial prowess.

The visit begins with a trip to the Vulcan Center, where you can explore interactive exhibits and displays that delve into the city's history and the significance of the iron and steel industry. The museum provides a comprehensive overview of Birmingham's development and the role it played during the late 19th and early 20th centuries.

Ascending to the observation balcony, you're treated to a breathtaking view of the city skyline and its surrounding landscapes. The vantage point from Vulcan Park allows you to appreciate the geographical layout of Birmingham, from the urban areas to the natural beauty of the surrounding hills.

The centerpiece of Vulcan Park is, of course, the Vulcan statue. This colossal figure stands at 56 feet and is perched on a pedestal that brings it to an elevation of 180 feet above the city. The statue itself represents the Roman god of fire and the forge, symbolizing Birmingham's historical association with the iron and steel industry.

Surrounding the park are beautifully landscaped grounds, making it an ideal spot for a leisurely stroll or a picnic. The park often hosts events and concerts, contributing to its role as a community gathering space.

Vulcan Park and Museum is not only a tribute to Birmingham's industrial heritage but also a venue for cultural events and educational programs. The site's commitment to preserving its historical significance while embracing contemporary uses makes it a dynamic destination for locals and visitors alike.

Whether you're interested in history, seeking a picturesque view of Birmingham, or simply looking for a relaxing outdoor space, a visit to Vulcan Park and

Museum offers a multi-faceted experience that celebrates the city's past and present. It's a must-see destination that combines cultural enrichment with the natural beauty of Red Mountain.

# 15.Explore the McWane Science Center.

Exploring the McWane Science Center is an engaging and interactive adventure that combines education with fun, making it an ideal destination for visitors of all ages. Located in downtown Birmingham, the McWane Science Center is a dynamic hub for hands-on learning experiences, interactive exhibits, and immersive demonstrations.

The science center is divided into various thematic zones, each offering a unique exploration of scientific principles and phenomena. From the wonders of the human body in the "Itty Bitty Magic City" exhibit to the mysteries of space and astronomy in the "World of Water" exhibit, McWane Science Center covers a broad spectrum of scientific disciplines.

For those fascinated by dinosaurs and prehistoric life, the "Alabama Dinosaurs" exhibit provides a journey through the state's paleontological history. The center's commitment to making science accessible is evident in its interactive displays, encouraging visitors to actively participate and learn through hands-on experimentation.

The "IMAX Dome" theater at McWane Science Center adds another dimension to the experience, offering immersive screenings of educational films and documentaries. The theater's cutting-edge technology provides a visually stunning and educational cinematic experience.

One of the highlights for younger visitors is the "Just Mice Size" exhibit, a miniature city where children can play and explore various professions, fostering creativity and imaginative play.

McWane Science Center's commitment to community engagement is further emphasized through its educational programs, workshops, and special events. Whether it's a science demonstration, a themed workshop, or a live science show, there's always something happening to inspire curiosity and learning.

The science center is not just for children; adults can also enjoy the diverse range of exhibits and activities. The McWane Science Center creates an environment where curiosity is encouraged, making it an ideal destination for families, school groups, and anyone eager to explore the wonders of science in a hands-on and entertaining way.

# 16.Attend the Sidewalk Film Festival.

Attending the Sidewalk Film Festival is a cinematic and cultural experience that celebrates independent filmmaking in the vibrant city of Birmingham. Established in 1999, this annual event has become a cornerstone of the city's arts scene, drawing filmmakers, industry professionals, and film enthusiasts from across the country.

The Sidewalk Film Festival showcases a diverse selection of independent films, including documentaries, narrative features, shorts, and experimental works. The festival's commitment to highlighting emerging voices and unique perspectives in filmmaking contributes to its reputation as a platform for innovative storytelling.

The festival takes place in various venues throughout downtown Birmingham, creating a dynamic atmosphere that allows attendees to explore different parts of the city while enjoying a rich cinematic lineup. From historic theaters to outdoor screening spaces, each venue adds its own unique charm to the festival experience.

In addition to film screenings, the Sidewalk Film Festival features panel discussions, Q&A sessions with filmmakers, and special events that provide opportunities for interaction and dialogue. This creates a sense of community among attendees and fosters a deeper appreciation for the art of filmmaking.

One of the distinctive aspects of the Sidewalk Film Festival is its emphasis on accessibility and inclusivity. The festival aims to bring filmmakers and audiences together, fostering a spirit of collaboration and support within the independent film community.

Attending the Sidewalk Film Festival allows you to not only enjoy a diverse selection of films but also to engage with the filmmakers, industry professionals, and fellow film enthusiasts. The festival's impact extends beyond the screen, contributing to Birmingham's cultural landscape and reinforcing the city's reputation as a hub for creativity and artistic expression. It's an event that brings people together to celebrate the power of storytelling and the art of independent filmmaking in a welcoming and lively atmosphere.

# 17. Visit the Negro Southern League Museum.

Visiting the Negro Southern League Museum is a profoundly enriching experience that provides deep insights into the history and contributions of African American baseball players, particularly within the context of the Southern United States. Located in Birmingham, Alabama, the museum is dedicated to preserving and celebrating the legacy of the Negro Southern League, shedding light on the challenges and triumphs faced by black baseball players during a pivotal period in American history.

Upon entering the museum, visitors are greeted with a wealth of exhibits and displays that chronicle the rich history of the Negro Southern League. The museum showcases an array of artifacts, photographs, and memorabilia, offering a tangible connection to the stories of African American athletes who played a crucial role in the sport during a time of segregation.

One of the museum's standout features is the Hall of Fame, which honors and pays tribute to legendary players, coaches, and contributors from the Negro Leagues. This section serves as a testament to the talent, resilience, and trailblazing spirit of individuals who, despite facing systemic racism, made significant contributions to the world of baseball.

Throughout the museum, interactive displays and multimedia presentations provide a dynamic and engaging learning experience. Visitors can gain a deeper understanding of the social and cultural context in which the Negro Southern League operated, exploring the broader impact of baseball within African American communities and its role in breaking down racial barriers.

The Negro Southern League Museum also serves as an educational resource, offering programs and initiatives to promote awareness and understanding of this important chapter in American sports history. It is a place where visitors can reflect on the challenges and achievements of the past while recognizing the resilience and determination of those who paved the way for future generations.

In summary, a visit to the Negro Southern League Museum is a powerful and educational journey that not only honors the legacy of African American baseball players but also contributes to a broader understanding of the social and cultural dynamics that shaped American sports. It is a museum that celebrates diversity, inclusion, and the enduring spirit of those who made significant strides in the face of adversity.

# 18.Check out the murals in the Avondale neighborhood.

Checking out the murals in the Avondale neighborhood is a vibrant and artistic exploration that immerses visitors in the creative spirit of this dynamic area in Birmingham. Avondale, known for its eclectic atmosphere and diverse community, is adorned with colorful and expressive murals that contribute to the neighborhood's unique character.

Wandering through the streets of Avondale, you'll encounter an array of murals that showcase the talent and creativity of local and visiting artists. These outdoor artworks often reflect the cultural diversity, history, and community spirit of the neighborhood. From large-scale, intricate pieces to smaller, hidden gems, the murals in Avondale add a dynamic visual element to the urban landscape.

One notable area for mural exploration is along 41st Street South, where several businesses and walls serve as canvases for artistic expression. The vibrant colors and diverse themes of the murals contribute to the neighborhood's lively and welcoming atmosphere. Be sure to check out the details, as many murals convey messages, tell stories, or celebrate local culture.

In addition to the visual appeal, the murals in Avondale often serve as a backdrop for community events, festivals, and gatherings. The street art scene has become an integral part of the neighborhood's identity, attracting locals and visitors alike.

As you explore Avondale's murals, take the time to appreciate the eclectic mix of shops, restaurants, and cafes that contribute to the area's creative and bohemian vibe. The murals, combined with the diverse offerings of the neighborhood, create a unique and engaging experience for those who appreciate art, culture, and the sense of community.

Whether you're a street art enthusiast, a casual observer, or someone looking to soak in the local atmosphere, checking out the murals in the Avondale neighborhood is a visually stimulating and culturally enriching activity in the heart of Birmingham.

# 19.Have a picnic at Linn Park.

Having a picnic at Linn Park is a delightful and relaxing way to enjoy the outdoors in the heart of downtown Birmingham. Linn Park, named after Birmingham's founder, Charles Linn, is a green oasis that provides a peaceful escape from the urban hustle and bustle. Here's how you can make the most of your picnic experience:

1. Choose a Scenic Spot: Linn Park offers various scenic areas, from open lawns to shaded groves. Choose a spot that suits your preferences—whether you prefer a sunny area for warmth or a shaded spot for a cooler picnic.

2. Pack Your Picnic: Prepare a picnic basket with your favorite snacks, sandwiches, fruits, and refreshing beverages. Don't forget essentials like a blanket, napkins, and utensils. Consider bringing a mix of savory and sweet treats to satisfy your taste buds.

3. Relax and Enjoy: Once you've found the perfect spot, spread out your blanket, arrange your picnic spread, and take in the tranquil surroundings. Linn Park's central location makes it a convenient and accessible place for a leisurely outdoor meal.

4. People-Watching: Linn Park is a popular gathering place, and picnicking provides an excellent opportunity for people-watching. Observe locals enjoying the park, families playing, or perhaps catch a live performance or event if there's one taking place.

5. Explore the Park: After your picnic, take a leisurely stroll through the park. Explore the walking paths, admire the greenery, and discover any public art installations or historical monuments scattered throughout the park.

6. Capture Memories: Bring a camera or your smartphone to capture moments from your picnic. Whether it's a snapshot of your picnic spread, a scenic view, or candid shots of your time in the park, these photos can serve as lasting memories.

7. Check for Events: Linn Park often hosts events, festivals, and performances. Before planning your picnic, check if there are any upcoming activities that you might want to coincide with your visit for an added layer of entertainment.

Having a picnic at Linn Park provides a simple yet enjoyable outdoor experience, making it a wonderful way to connect with nature and unwind in the heart of downtown Birmingham.

# 20.Explore the Birmingham Zoo.

Exploring the Birmingham Zoo is an exciting and educational adventure that allows visitors to connect with a diverse range of animal species in a well-curated and immersive environment. Located in Birmingham's historic Lane Park, the zoo offers a captivating experience for individuals and families alike. Here's how you can make the most of your visit:

1. Discover Animal Habitats: The Birmingham Zoo is home to a variety of animals from around the world. Begin your exploration by visiting different habitats, such as the African savanna, Asian forest, and South American rainforest. Each area is designed to mimic the natural environments of the animals, providing a glimpse into their daily lives.

2. Attend Animal Encounters: Check the zoo's schedule for animal encounters, demonstrations, and feeding sessions. These interactive experiences offer valuable insights into the behaviors and characteristics of various species. It's an opportunity to learn more about conservation efforts and the importance of protecting wildlife.

3. Visit the Predator Zone: Explore the Predator Zone, where you can encounter big cats, bears, and other predators. The exhibits are designed to provide a safe and educational experience while allowing visitors to observe these majestic animals up close.

4. Engage with the Children's Zoo: If you're visiting with kids, don't miss the Children's Zoo area. This section is designed to be interactive, with opportunities for children to pet and feed animals, play in engaging exhibits, and learn about the importance of wildlife conservation in a kid-friendly environment.

5. Enjoy the Lorikeet Aviary: Step into the Lorikeet Aviary, where you can feed nectar to colorful lorikeet birds. It's a unique and immersive experience that allows you to interact with these vibrant and social birds in a lush tropical setting.

6. Explore the Alabama Wilds: The Alabama Wilds exhibit showcases the native wildlife of Alabama, providing insight into the state's diverse ecosystems. It's a chance to appreciate and learn about the animals that call the region home.

7. Plan for Special Events: Check the zoo's calendar for special events, seasonal exhibits, and themed activities. The Birmingham Zoo often hosts events like Boo at the Zoo during Halloween or special holiday-themed attractions.

8. Take a Break: The zoo offers picnic areas and spots for relaxation. Bring snacks or enjoy a meal from the on-site cafe, and take a moment to recharge before continuing your exploration.

Visiting the Birmingham Zoo offers not only a fun and entertaining experience but also an opportunity to support conservation efforts and learn about the importance of protecting the planet's biodiversity. Whether you're a wildlife enthusiast, a family with children, or someone looking for a day of outdoor enjoyment, the Birmingham Zoo provides a memorable and enriching experience.

# 21.Take a historic walking tour of the city.

Embarking on a historic walking tour of Birmingham is a fascinating journey through time, allowing you to explore the city's rich history, cultural landmarks, and architectural gems. Here's a suggested itinerary for your walking tour:

1. Start at Linn Park:
Begin your walking tour at Linn Park, the central green space named after Birmingham's founder, Charles Linn. While there, visit the Civil Rights Foot Soldiers Memorial and the Confederate Soldiers and Sailors Monument, gaining insights into Birmingham's complex history.

2. Birmingham Civil Rights District:
Head towards the Birmingham Civil Rights District, a significant area in the city's history. Visit the Birmingham Civil Rights Institute to explore exhibits that detail the struggles and triumphs of the civil rights movement. Don't miss

the nearby Kelly Ingram Park, adorned with sculptures and memorials commemorating pivotal events.

3. 16th Street Baptist Church:
Walk to the iconic 16th Street Baptist Church, a pivotal site in civil rights history. Learn about the tragic bombing in 1963 and the role of the church in the struggle for equality.

4. Alabama Theatre:
Head towards the historic Alabama Theatre, a beautifully preserved venue dating back to 1927. While you may not be able to take a tour inside, admire the exterior and learn about the theater's cultural significance.

5. McWane Science Center:
Continue your stroll to the McWane Science Center, housed in the historic Loveman's department store building. Although the focus is on science exhibits, the building itself is a testament to Birmingham's architectural heritage.

6. Morris Avenue:
Walk to Morris Avenue, one of Birmingham's oldest streets. Lined with historic buildings, this area provides a glimpse into the city's industrial past. Explore the cobblestone streets and appreciate the architecture.

7. The Heaviest Corner on Earth:
Head to the intersection of 20th Street and 1st Avenue North, known as "The Heaviest Corner on Earth." Marvel at the historic skyscrapers that once made this intersection a symbol of Birmingham's economic prosperity.

8. Five Points South:
Conclude your walking tour in the vibrant Five Points South district. This area is known for its eclectic mix of shops, restaurants, and historic architecture. Take a moment to relax and reflect on the historical journey you've undertaken.

Throughout your historic walking tour, be sure to observe the architecture, read historical markers, and immerse yourself in the stories that shaped Birmingham into the city it is today. Remember to check for guided tours or additional information at visitor centers to enhance your experience.

# 22.Attend the Moss Rock Festival.

Attending the Moss Rock Festival is a lively and culturally enriching experience that immerses you in the vibrant arts and environmental scene of Birmingham. Here's how you can make the most of your visit to this unique festival:

1. Explore Local Artisans:
Moss Rock Festival showcases a diverse array of local artisans and craftsmen. Wander through the artist booths to discover handmade crafts, jewelry, paintings, and other unique creations. Engage with the artists, learn about their creative processes, and perhaps find a special piece to take home.

2. Enjoy Live Music:
Check the festival schedule for live music performances. Many festivals, including Moss Rock, feature local and regional bands across various genres. Take a break from exploring and enjoy the tunes while soaking in the festive atmosphere.

3. Experience Nature and Conservation:
Moss Rock Festival often incorporates environmental and conservation themes. Attend eco-friendly workshops, learn about sustainable practices, and discover ways to connect with and protect the natural world. Engaging with environmental organizations and exhibits can be both educational and inspiring.

4. Bring the Family:
Moss Rock Festival is family-friendly, with activities for all ages. Look for kid-friendly zones, interactive exhibits, and hands-on activities that make the festival an enjoyable experience for families. It's a great opportunity to introduce children to the arts and environmental awareness.

5. Taste Local Cuisine:
Explore the food vendors and trucks to savor local cuisine. Many festivals celebrate the culinary diversity of the region, offering a chance to indulge in delicious treats and meals. Whether it's regional specialties or international flavors, Moss Rock Festival often provides a tasty culinary experience.

6. Participate in Workshops:
Check the festival schedule for workshops and demonstrations. These may include art workshops, gardening tips, or DIY sessions. Participating in these activities can add an interactive and educational dimension to your festival experience.

7. Embrace the Outdoors:
Moss Rock Festival often takes advantage of its scenic setting. Enjoy the outdoors by taking a stroll through Moss Rock Preserve, which features hiking trails and unique geological formations. The natural surroundings complement the festival's focus on art and environmental consciousness.

8. Plan Ahead:
Before attending, review the festival's schedule and map to identify specific areas or events you don't want to miss. Planning ahead ensures that you can make the most of your time and experience the full breadth of what Moss Rock Festival has to offer.

Attending the Moss Rock Festival is not just an event; it's an opportunity to engage with the local community, support local artists and environmental initiatives, and enjoy a festive atmosphere that celebrates the intersection of art and nature.

# 23. Walk along the Rotary Trail.

Walking along the Rotary Trail in Birmingham offers a scenic and recreational experience, providing a dynamic urban pathway that connects neighborhoods and showcases the city's commitment to outdoor spaces. Here's how you can make the most of your stroll along this vibrant trail:

1. Start at Railroad Park:
Begin your walk at Railroad Park, a central gathering place in downtown Birmingham. Explore the park's green spaces, water features, and sculptures before heading towards the Rotary Trail.

2. Access the Rotary Trail:
The Rotary Trail is accessible from Railroad Park, and you can easily transition from the park to the trail. Look for the trailhead markers and follow the path to embark on your walking adventure.

3. Enjoy Public Art:
As you walk along the Rotary Trail, appreciate the public art installations that enhance the urban landscape. Birmingham's commitment to incorporating art

into public spaces is evident along this trail, adding a creative and cultural element to your stroll.

4. Experience the Urban Scenery:
The Rotary Trail offers unique views of Birmingham's urban scenery. As you walk, take in the city skyline, observe architectural details, and enjoy the juxtaposition of nature and urban development.

5. Take a Break at Green Spaces:
The trail features green spaces and seating areas where you can take a break, relax, or have a picnic. Enjoy moments of tranquility amid the city's hustle and bustle.

6. Connect with Local Community:
The Rotary Trail serves as a community space, attracting locals and visitors alike. Engage with fellow walkers, joggers, and cyclists, fostering a sense of community along the trail.

7. Visit the Historic Rotary Trail Bridge:
Admire the historic Rotary Trail Bridge, a repurposed railroad bridge that spans the trail. The bridge adds a touch of history to your walk and offers picturesque views of the surrounding area.

8. Explore Nearby Neighborhoods:
Depending on your route, the Rotary Trail connects to neighborhoods such as Lakeview and Avondale. Consider extending your walk to explore these vibrant areas, known for their local shops, restaurants, and cultural attractions.

9. Capture the Sunset:
If your walk coincides with the evening, aim to catch the sunset along the Rotary Trail. The changing colors of the sky against the city backdrop create a picturesque and memorable scene.

10. Be Mindful of Events:
Check for any events or activities happening along the Rotary Trail, as the space is often utilized for community gatherings, fitness classes, or cultural events. Participating in these activities can add a dynamic element to your walk.

Walking along the Rotary Trail is not just about exercise; it's a chance to immerse yourself in Birmingham's urban environment, appreciate public art, and connect with the local community. Whether you're looking for a leisurely stroll, a scenic run, or a place to unwind, the Rotary Trail offers a versatile and accessible outdoor experience in the heart of the city.

# 24. Visit the Southern Museum of Flight.

Visiting the Southern Museum of Flight is an aviation enthusiast's dream, providing a comprehensive exploration of the history and evolution of flight. Located in Birmingham, Alabama, the museum showcases a diverse collection of aircraft, exhibits, and artifacts. Here's a suggested plan for making the most of your visit:

1. Explore the Exhibits:
Begin your visit by exploring the museum's exhibits. These exhibits cover various aspects of aviation, from the early days of flight to modern aerospace technology. Learn about the pioneers of aviation, the evolution of aircraft design, and the impact of aviation on society.

2. Marvel at Historic Aircraft:
The Southern Museum of Flight houses a remarkable collection of historic aircraft. Take your time to marvel at the different planes on display, each with its own unique story. From vintage biplanes to military jets, the museum provides a glimpse into the evolution of aviation technology.

3. Cockpit Simulators:
If available, consider trying out the cockpit simulators. These interactive experiences allow you to get a feel for what it's like to operate an aircraft. It's a hands-on opportunity to appreciate the skill and precision required in aviation.

4. Visit the Alabama Aviation Hall of Fame:
Explore the Alabama Aviation Hall of Fame, which honors individuals who have made significant contributions to aviation in the state. Learn about the achievements and legacies of these aviation pioneers.

5. Attend Special Events:
Check the museum's schedule for any special events or demonstrations. The Southern Museum of Flight often hosts educational programs, workshops, and airshows. Attending these events can enhance your overall experience and provide additional insights into aviation.

6. Gift Shop:
Don't forget to visit the museum's gift shop. Here, you can find aviation-themed souvenirs, books, and memorabilia. It's a great place to pick up a memento to commemorate your visit.

7. Learn About Military Aviation:
Explore exhibits dedicated to military aviation, showcasing the role of aircraft in various conflicts. Gain an understanding of the technological advancements that have shaped military aviation throughout history.

8. Outdoor Aircraft Display:
If the museum has an outdoor aircraft display, take some time to explore these planes as well. This could include larger aircraft that may not fit within the museum building.

9. Educational Programs:
If you have a specific interest in aviation, inquire about any educational programs or guided tours offered by the museum. These programs may provide a more in-depth exploration of certain topics or areas within the museum.

10. Plan Your Visit:
Before heading to the Southern Museum of Flight, check the museum's website for hours of operation, admission fees, and any special guidelines or events. Planning ahead ensures a smooth and enjoyable visit.

Visiting the Southern Museum of Flight offers a captivating journey through the history of aviation, making it an educational and inspiring destination for aviation enthusiasts and anyone curious about the wonders of flight.

# 25.Explore the Five Points South Historic District.

Exploring the Five Points South Historic District in Birmingham is a delightful journey through a vibrant and eclectic neighborhood with a rich history. Here's a suggested itinerary to make the most of your visit:

1. Start at Brother Bryan Park:

Begin your exploration at Brother Bryan Park, a charming green space named after a beloved local pastor. Enjoy the serene atmosphere, relax on a bench, and take in the surroundings before venturing further into Five Points South.

2. Historic Architecture:
Wander through the streets of Five Points South to appreciate the district's historic architecture. The area is known for its diverse architectural styles, including Colonial Revival, Tudor, and Craftsman homes. Keep an eye out for unique details and well-preserved structures.

3. Five Points Fountain:
Head to the iconic Five Points Fountain, a central landmark in the district. The fountain serves as a meeting point and a hub of activity. Admire the sculpture and the vibrant energy of the area.

4. Dining and Shopping:
Five Points South is renowned for its diverse dining scene and unique boutiques. Explore the multitude of restaurants, cafes, and shops that line the streets. Whether you're in the mood for international cuisine, a cozy coffee shop, or stylish boutiques, Five Points South has something for every taste.

5. Highland Avenue:
Stroll along Highland Avenue, one of the main thoroughfares in the district. This bustling street is lined with historic buildings, trendy eateries, and a mix of local businesses.

6. The Pickwick Plaza:
Visit the Pickwick Plaza, an architectural gem that has been a focal point of Five Points South since the early 20th century. This historic building adds character to the district and often hosts events or houses popular establishments.

7. Vulcan Park and Museum:
While not directly in Five Points South, Vulcan Park and Museum is nearby. Consider extending your exploration to visit this iconic Birmingham landmark. The park offers panoramic views of the city, and the Vulcan statue is a symbol of Birmingham's industrial heritage.

8. Entertainment Venues:
Five Points South is a hub for entertainment. Check out the district's live music venues, theaters, or comedy clubs for a dose of local culture and entertainment.

9. Take a Break at a Park or Courtyard:
If you need a break, find a cozy park or courtyard to relax in. Five Points South has several hidden gems, providing tranquil spaces amidst the urban setting.

10. Attend a Local Event:
Check the local events calendar for any festivals, markets, or community events happening in Five Points South. Attending a local event can add a dynamic and festive element to your visit.

Exploring the Five Points South Historic District allows you to immerse yourself in Birmingham's cultural and culinary scene while appreciating the charm of a neighborhood steeped in history. Whether you're drawn to historic architecture, vibrant street life, or eclectic dining options, Five Points South offers a diverse and engaging experience.

# 26.Attend a UAB Blazers basketball game.

Attending a UAB Blazers basketball game is an exciting way to experience the spirited atmosphere of college sports and support the University of Alabama at Birmingham's athletic teams. Here's how you can make the most of your visit:

1. Check the Schedule:
Before planning your visit, check the UAB Blazers basketball schedule to find a game that fits your schedule. You can find the schedule on the official UAB Athletics website or through other reputable sports platforms.

2. Purchase Tickets:
Once you've identified a game you'd like to attend, purchase your tickets in advance. You can buy tickets online through the official UAB Athletics website or at the venue on game day if available.

3. Wear Team Colors:
Show your support for the UAB Blazers by wearing the team colors—green and gold. It adds to the overall game day experience and demonstrates your enthusiasm for the team.

4. Arrive Early:
Arrive at the venue early to soak in the pre-game atmosphere. You can explore the arena, grab some team merchandise, and enjoy the buzz of anticipation before the game begins.

5. Experience the Spirit:
College basketball games are known for their spirited atmospheres. Join in the cheers, chants, and school spirit as the UAB Blazers take to the court. Engage with fellow fans and become part of the enthusiastic crowd.

6. Enjoy Concessions:
Indulge in the classic game day experience by trying the concessions at the arena. Whether it's a hot dog, nachos, or your favorite stadium snack, savoring these treats adds to the overall enjoyment of the game.

7. Participate in Game Day Activities:
Check if there are any special game day activities or promotions. Some games may feature halftime performances, giveaways, or other entertaining events to enhance the overall fan experience.

8. Familiarize Yourself with the Team:
Brush up on the UAB Blazers' basketball team roster, key players, and recent performances. Having some knowledge about the team adds to your appreciation of the game and makes it more engaging.

9. Capture the Moment:
Bring your camera or smartphone to capture memorable moments during the game. Whether it's a crucial play, the excitement of the crowd, or a celebratory moment, these snapshots will serve as lasting memories of your experience.

10. Stay Until the End:
To fully experience the game day atmosphere, stay until the end of the match. Enjoy post-game celebrations, acknowledgments, and perhaps even the chance to meet some of the players or coaches.

Attending a UAB Blazers basketball game is not just about the sport—it's a chance to immerse yourself in the collegiate sports culture, connect with fellow fans, and cheer for the home team. Whether you're a passionate basketball enthusiast or a casual sports fan, the energy and camaraderie at a UAB Blazers game make it a memorable and enjoyable experience.

# 27. Take a brewery tour in the Avondale Brewing District.

Embarking on a brewery tour in the Avondale Brewing District is a fantastic way to explore Birmingham's craft beer scene and experience the unique charm of this revitalized neighborhood. Here's a suggested itinerary for your brewery tour:

1. Avondale Brewing Company:
Start your brewery tour at the Avondale Brewing Company, one of the pioneers in the district. Explore the brewery's taproom and outdoor spaces while enjoying a flight of their craft beers. Avondale Brewing Company often features a diverse range of brews, so take your time to savor the flavors.

2. Post Office Pies:
While not a brewery, Post Office Pies, located nearby, is a popular spot for pizza and craft beer. Consider making it your next stop for a delicious meal paired with a selection of local and regional brews.

3. Good People Brewing Company:
Continue your tour with a visit to the Good People Brewing Company. Known for its commitment to quality and sustainability, Good People offers a variety of craft beers. Take a brewery tour if available to gain insights into the brewing process and the brewery's ethos.

4. Hop City Beer & Wine:
Make a pit stop at Hop City Beer & Wine, a craft beer store with a vast selection of local and international brews. It's an excellent place to pick up some unique beers to enjoy later or to take home as souvenirs.

5. Cahaba Brewing Company:
Conclude your brewery tour at Cahaba Brewing Company. Known for its laid-back atmosphere and a range of beer styles, Cahaba Brewing offers a great setting to relax and reflect on your brewery-hopping adventure.

6. Enjoy Outdoor Spaces:
Many of the breweries in the Avondale Brewing District have outdoor spaces, patios, or beer gardens. Take advantage of the Alabama weather by enjoying your beers in these inviting outdoor areas.

7. Explore Avondale:

Between brewery stops, take some time to explore the Avondale neighborhood. The district is known for its street art, unique shops, and local character. A leisurely stroll adds to the overall experience of the brewery tour.

8. Plan for Events:
Check the schedules of the breweries for any special events, live music, or brewery tours that might coincide with your visit. Participating in brewery events can enhance your overall experience and provide additional entertainment.

9. Drink Responsibly:
As with any brewery tour, it's essential to drink responsibly. Consider arranging transportation in advance, whether it's a designated driver, rideshare service, or public transportation.

10. Support Local Businesses:
Throughout your brewery tour, take the opportunity to support local businesses. Whether it's enjoying a meal at a nearby restaurant or purchasing brewery merchandise, contributing to the local economy adds to the positive impact of your visit.

A brewery tour in the Avondale Brewing District offers a dynamic blend of craft beer, local culture, and community spirit. It's an opportunity to taste unique brews, explore a revitalized neighborhood, and connect with the vibrant craft beer scene in Birmingham.

# 28.Experience the Birmingham Ghost Walk.

Participating in the Birmingham Ghost Walk is an intriguing and spine-chilling way to explore the city's haunted history and mysterious tales. Here's a suggested plan for experiencing the Birmingham Ghost Walk:

1. Check the Schedule:
Before planning your ghost walk, check the schedule of the Birmingham Ghost Walk. Ensure that the walk is available on the date you plan to attend, and make any necessary reservations or bookings.

2. Dress Comfortably:

Wear comfortable clothing and shoes suitable for walking, as the ghost walk typically involves exploring different parts of the city on foot. Check the weather forecast to dress appropriately for the conditions.

3. Arrive Early:
Arrive at the meeting point early to ensure a smooth check-in process and to have time to chat with the guide or fellow participants. This also allows you to soak in the atmosphere of the starting location.

4. Engage with the Guide:
Interact with the guide leading the ghost walk. They often have fascinating stories and historical information to share. Don't hesitate to ask questions and engage in the spooky tales unfolding during the tour.

5. Explore Haunted Sites:
Follow the guide as they lead you to various haunted sites and locations with ghostly stories. Listen attentively to the eerie tales and legends associated with each spot. Many ghost walks feature landmarks, historic buildings, and areas with reported paranormal activity.

6. Capture the Atmosphere:
Bring a camera or smartphone to capture the atmosphere and any interesting sights during the ghost walk. Some tours may even encourage participants to share their ghostly photos or experiences.

7. Stay Open-Minded:
Keep an open mind throughout the ghost walk. While the stories may be spooky and entertaining, approach the experience with a sense of curiosity and intrigue rather than skepticism.

8. Respect Historic Sites:
Remember that some of the locations visited on the ghost walk may be historic sites or private properties. Be respectful of the surroundings and follow any guidelines or rules provided by the guide.

9. Attend with a Group:
Consider attending the ghost walk with a group of friends or family. Sharing the experience with others can add to the fun and make the spooky tales more enjoyable.

10. Reflect on the Experience:

After the ghost walk, take some time to reflect on the experience. Discuss the stories you heard, share your thoughts with fellow participants, and perhaps explore any historical aspects that piqued your interest.

Participating in the Birmingham Ghost Walk offers a unique blend of history, folklore, and the paranormal. Whether you're a believer in ghost stories or just looking for a thrilling evening adventure, the ghost walk provides a memorable and atmospheric exploration of Birmingham's haunted past.

# 29.Attend the Birmingham Greek Festival.

Attending the Birmingham Greek Festival is a delightful way to immerse yourself in Greek culture, savor authentic cuisine, and experience the vibrant atmosphere of this annual event. Here's a suggested plan for making the most of your visit to the Birmingham Greek Festival:

1. Check the Festival Dates:
Before planning your visit, check the official dates of the Birmingham Greek Festival. The festival is usually held annually, and confirming the schedule ensures you don't miss out on this cultural celebration.

2. Arrive Early:
Arrive at the festival early to avoid crowds and have the opportunity to explore the offerings at a leisurely pace. Early arrival allows you to participate in various activities and enjoy the festival's ambiance.

3. Explore the Food Offerings:
Greek festivals are renowned for their delicious and authentic cuisine. Explore the food booths and indulge in classic Greek dishes such as moussaka, souvlaki, gyros, baklava, and more. Don't forget to pair your meal with a refreshing glass of Greek wine or traditional beverages.

4. Enjoy Live Entertainment:
Check the festival schedule for live performances featuring traditional Greek music and dance. Take a seat, relax, and enjoy the lively entertainment that adds to the festive atmosphere.

5. Visit the Marketplace:

Explore the marketplace, where you can find a variety of Greek products, crafts, and souvenirs. From handmade jewelry to Greek olive oil, the marketplace offers a chance to take home a piece of Greek culture.

6. Participate in Cultural Activities:
Engage in any cultural activities or workshops that may be offered during the festival. This could include dance lessons, cooking demonstrations, or art displays that provide insights into Greek traditions.

7. Learn About Greek Heritage:
Attend presentations or exhibits that showcase the rich history and heritage of Greece. Whether it's information about famous landmarks, mythology, or cultural practices, learning more about Greek heritage adds depth to your festival experience.

8. Support Local Organizations:
The Birmingham Greek Festival is often organized by local Greek communities or churches. Take the opportunity to support these organizations by purchasing food, crafts, or merchandise. Your contribution helps sustain and promote cultural events in the community.

9. Embrace the Greek Hospitality:
Greek festivals are known for their warm hospitality. Engage with festival volunteers, learn about Greek customs, and embrace the friendly atmosphere. Don't hesitate to ask questions or strike up conversations to enhance your cultural experience.

10. Capture Memories:
Bring a camera or smartphone to capture memories of your time at the Birmingham Greek Festival. Document the vibrant colors, traditional attire, and the joyous moments to reminisce about this cultural celebration.

Attending the Birmingham Greek Festival offers a sensory and cultural experience, allowing you to savor the flavors, sounds, and traditions of Greece right in the heart of Birmingham. Whether you're a food enthusiast, a lover of cultural events, or someone looking for a festive atmosphere, this annual celebration is a must-attend for those interested in Greek culture.

# 30.Explore the Pepper Place Saturday Market.

Exploring the Pepper Place Saturday Market is a delightful way to experience the vibrant local culture, support regional farmers and artisans, and enjoy a diverse array of fresh produce and handmade goods. Here's a suggested plan for making the most of your visit to the Pepper Place Saturday Market:

1. Arrive Early:
Start your day by arriving early at the market. This allows you to beat the crowds and enjoy a leisurely exploration of the various vendors and offerings.

2. Browse Fresh Produce:
Begin your market journey by perusing the fresh produce stands. Local farmers and vendors offer a colorful array of fruits, vegetables, and herbs. Take your time to select the freshest and seasonal items.

3. Sample Local Treats:
Explore the market's food vendors and sample local treats and specialties. Whether it's artisanal cheeses, baked goods, or prepared foods, indulging in these local flavors adds to the culinary experience.

4. Support Artisans:
Wander through the artisan stalls featuring handmade crafts, jewelry, and unique products. This is an excellent opportunity to support local artists and find one-of-a-kind treasures.

5. Enjoy Live Entertainment:
Check the market schedule for live entertainment. Many markets feature musicians, performers, or even cooking demonstrations that enhance the overall atmosphere.

6. Grab a Coffee:
If the market includes coffee vendors, treat yourself to a cup of freshly brewed coffee. It's a perfect pick-me-up as you continue exploring the market.

7. Interact with Farmers and Vendors:
Strike up conversations with local farmers and vendors. Learn about their products, farming practices, and the stories behind their businesses. Building these connections adds a personal touch to your market experience.

8. Bring a Reusable Bag:
Come prepared with a reusable bag to carry your purchases. Not only does this help you stay organized, but it's also an eco-friendly choice that aligns with the sustainability ethos often found at farmers' markets.

9. Explore Nearby Shops:
If the market is situated in an area with local shops, take some time to explore the surrounding neighborhood. You might discover boutique stores, art galleries, or additional dining options.

10. Plan for Breakfast or Brunch:
Consider planning your visit around breakfast or brunch time. Some markets have food vendors offering delicious breakfast options, allowing you to enjoy a meal as part of your market experience.

11. Check for Seasonal Events:
Be aware of any seasonal events or themed markets that may coincide with your visit. Seasonal markets often feature special activities, celebrations, or additional vendors based on the time of year.

12. Capture the Market Vibes:
Bring a camera or smartphone to capture the vibrant colors, unique displays, and lively atmosphere of the market. Documenting your visit allows you to relive the experience and share it with others.

The Pepper Place Saturday Market provides an opportunity to engage with the local community, savor fresh and seasonal produce, and discover the creativity of local artisans. Whether you're a food enthusiast, a supporter of sustainable practices, or someone looking for a lively weekend activity, the market offers a dynamic and enriching experience.

# 31.Take a bike ride along the Jones Valley Trail.

Embarking on a bike ride along the Jones Valley Trail is an immersive journey into the heart of Birmingham's natural beauty and urban charm. As you set out, the well-maintained paths of the trail guide you through the picturesque landscapes of Jones Valley, offering a perfect blend of lush greenery and city vistas. The trail winds its way along scenic routes, providing cyclists with a diverse and engaging terrain to explore.

Begin your ride with a sense of anticipation, absorbing the fresh air and the rhythmic hum of your bicycle. The trail's design caters to cyclists of varying skill levels, making it an accessible and enjoyable route for both beginners and seasoned riders. The careful integration of nature and urban elements along the trail ensures that you experience the dynamic character of Birmingham.

Pedal at your own pace, allowing yourself to be captivated by the changing scenery. Pass by serene pockets of nature, urban parks, and perhaps even catch glimpses of local landmarks. The Jones Valley Trail is not just a path; it's a passage through Birmingham's history and development, offering a unique perspective on the city's past and present.

Take breaks along the way to appreciate designated rest areas or scenic viewpoints. These pauses not only provide moments of respite but also allow you to fully immerse yourself in the surroundings. Bring along a water bottle to stay hydrated, and perhaps a camera to capture the visual poetry of the trail—the play of light through the leaves, the urban architecture juxtaposed with nature, and the vibrant hues that change with the seasons.

Consider planning your ride during different times of the day or seasons to witness the trail's transformative beauty. Whether it's the golden hues of a sunrise ride or the cool shadows cast by the afternoon sun, each moment on the Jones Valley Trail unveils a new facet of Birmingham's charm.

As you reach the conclusion of your bike ride, take a moment to reflect on the physical and mental rejuvenation that comes from cycling through such a diverse and thoughtfully crafted trail. The Jones Valley Trail not only offers a recreational outlet but also serves as a testament to the city's commitment to providing its residents and visitors with accessible, enjoyable, and nature-infused spaces.

# 32. Attend a performance at the Alys Stephens Performing Arts Center.

Attending a performance at the Alys Stephens Performing Arts Center is an immersive and culturally enriching experience. As you make your way to this state-of-the-art venue, anticipation builds for the artistic journey that awaits. The

Alys Stephens Center, with its modern architecture and world-class facilities, stands as a beacon for the arts in Birmingham.

Upon entering the center, you are greeted by an atmosphere of sophistication and creativity. The venue's commitment to providing a diverse range of performances, from classical concerts to contemporary productions, ensures there's something for every artistic palate.

Take the time to explore the lobby, adorned with elegant decor and perhaps housing exhibits or displays related to the performance. The center's dedication to creating a holistic experience extends beyond the stage, offering patrons an opportunity to engage with the arts on multiple levels.

As the performance begins, settle into the comfortable seating and let the magic unfold before you. The acoustics and lighting design of the Alys Stephens Center contribute to an immersive and impactful presentation, whether it be a symphony, theatrical production, dance performance, or any other artistic expression.

Throughout the performance, allow yourself to be transported into the narrative or emotion conveyed by the artists. The stage becomes a canvas, and the performers, masters of their craft, bring stories and emotions to life. The Alys Stephens Center's commitment to curating a diverse lineup ensures that each visit can offer a new and unique artistic encounter.

Consider checking the center's schedule in advance to align your visit with a performance that resonates with your interests. After the show, take a moment to appreciate the cultural significance of the experience and, if possible, explore any post-performance events or discussions that may enhance your connection with the artistic community.

Attending a performance at the Alys Stephens Performing Arts Center is not just about witnessing a show; it's about becoming part of a cultural celebration, supporting the arts community, and relishing the transformative power of live performances. Whether you're a seasoned arts enthusiast or someone discovering the magic of the stage, the Alys Stephens Center promises an unforgettable and enriching experience in the heart of Birmingham.

# 33.Explore the Historic Rickwood Field.

Exploring Historic Rickwood Field is a journey back in time, a chance to step onto the hallowed grounds where baseball history was made. As you approach the ballpark, the iconic façade and vintage architecture transport you to an era when baseball was more than a sport—it was a cultural phenomenon. Rickwood Field, nestled in Birmingham, holds the distinction of being one of the oldest baseball parks in the United States.

Upon entering the ballpark, the aura of nostalgia is palpable. The wooden grandstand, the meticulously maintained field, and the echoes of games played decades ago create an atmosphere steeped in the rich traditions of America's pastime. Take a leisurely stroll around the stands, envisioning the roaring crowds, the crack of the bat, and the cheers that once reverberated through this historic venue.

Rickwood Field's history is intertwined with the legendary players who graced its diamond, making it a storied landmark. Pause at points of historical significance, such as the plaques commemorating notable moments, and absorb the tales of baseball greats who competed on this field.

The authenticity of the stadium is evident in every detail—the manually operated scoreboard, the weathered wooden seats, and the nostalgic advertisements that adorn the outfield fence. These elements contribute to the timelessness of the ballpark, preserving its heritage for future generations.

Consider planning your visit during special events, such as vintage baseball games or annual Rickwood Classic events, which provide an immersive experience into the bygone eras of the sport. Attendees often don period-appropriate attire, further enhancing the retro ambiance and celebrating the enduring spirit of Rickwood Field.

Whether you're a baseball enthusiast, a history buff, or simply someone appreciating the cultural significance of well-preserved landmarks, exploring Historic Rickwood Field is a captivating experience. It's a chance to connect with the roots of America's favorite pastime and to appreciate the enduring legacy of a venue that has witnessed the evolution of baseball for over a century.

# 34.Attend the Magic City Art Connection.

# Travel to Birmingham Alabama

Attending the Magic City Art Connection is an immersive and vibrant experience that allows you to explore the diverse world of visual arts, connect with local and national artists, and engage with Birmingham's dynamic cultural scene. As you make your way to the event, the anticipation builds for the artistic discoveries that await.

Upon entering the festival grounds, you're greeted by a kaleidoscope of colors, a symphony of creative energy, and an array of artistic expressions. The Magic City Art Connection, held in the heart of Birmingham, showcases a broad spectrum of visual arts, including paintings, sculptures, photography, and mixed-media works.

Wander through the artist booths, each one a mini-gallery featuring the unique perspectives and talents of a myriad of artists. Take the time to interact with the creators, gaining insights into their creative processes and the inspiration behind their works. The festival provides a rare opportunity to engage directly with artists, fostering a deeper appreciation for the stories woven into each piece.

Explore the various mediums on display, from traditional to contemporary, and witness the convergence of different artistic styles. The festival's commitment to diversity ensures that there's something for everyone, whether you're a seasoned art enthusiast or someone discovering the joy of visual expression.

Immerse yourself in the interactive art experiences and installations that may be scattered throughout the festival. These hands-on activities often add an element of participation, inviting attendees to be a part of the artistic process.

Enjoy live performances and entertainment, from music to dance, enhancing the overall festive atmosphere. The Magic City Art Connection isn't just about static exhibits; it's a dynamic celebration of creativity, where the arts come to life in various forms.

Consider indulging in culinary delights from local food vendors or relaxing in designated seating areas, soaking in the ambiance of the event. The fusion of art, music, and community creates a lively and welcoming atmosphere.

Support the artists by considering a purchase or simply expressing appreciation for their work. Many artists showcase exclusive pieces at the festival, providing an opportunity to bring home a unique and meaningful memento of your experience.

Before leaving, check the festival's schedule for any workshops, talks, or demonstrations. These additional offerings can deepen your understanding of the artistic processes and provide valuable insights into the creative community.

Attending the Magic City Art Connection is not just a visit to an art festival; it's an invitation to immerse yourself in the vibrant and ever-evolving tapestry of Birmingham's cultural landscape. Whether you're an art collector, a casual observer, or someone seeking inspiration, the Magic City Art Connection promises a day filled with creativity, exploration, and a celebration of the arts.

# 35. Visit the Birmingham Civil Rights National Monument.

Visiting the Birmingham Civil Rights National Monument is a powerful and poignant journey into the heart of the civil rights movement in the United States. As you approach the monument, located in downtown Birmingham, a sense of historical significance and reverence envelops you. The site itself holds deep meaning, symbolizing the struggle for equality and justice during a pivotal era in American history.

Start your exploration at the visitor center, where you can gain insights into the historical context, events, and figures associated with the civil rights movement in Birmingham. Exhibits, multimedia presentations, and artifacts provide a comprehensive overview, setting the stage for a meaningful visit.

Step outside to the Kelly Ingram Park, adjacent to the monument, where powerful sculptures and installations commemorate the bravery and resilience of those who fought for civil rights. The park's design integrates art and history, creating a moving outdoor museum that invites reflection on the challenges faced and the progress made.

As you stand before the 16th Street Baptist Church, a prominent feature of the monument, reflect on its pivotal role in the civil rights struggle. The church serves as a poignant reminder of the tragic bombing in 1963, which claimed the lives of four African American girls and galvanized the nation's commitment to change.

Walk along the historic 16th Street, known as "Freedom Walk," where significant events unfolded during the civil rights protests. The street bears witness to the marches, demonstrations, and confrontations that defined Birmingham's role in the movement.

Consider participating in a guided tour, if available, to gain deeper insights into the specific locations within the monument. Knowledgeable guides can provide historical context, share personal stories, and help you connect emotionally with the profound impact of the civil rights struggle.

Take time to absorb the atmosphere and pay homage to the individuals who courageously fought against segregation and discrimination. The Birmingham Civil Rights National Monument serves as a testament to the resilience of the human spirit and the ongoing journey toward justice and equality.

Before leaving, visit the Birmingham Civil Rights Institute, which complements the monument by offering a more extensive exploration of the civil rights movement. The institute houses exhibits, archives, and educational programs that further enrich your understanding of this crucial chapter in American history.

Visiting the Birmingham Civil Rights National Monument is not just a historical excursion; it's an opportunity to engage with the legacy of those who paved the way for civil rights and social justice. It's a chance to reflect on the progress made and the ongoing commitment to building a more inclusive and equitable society.

# 36. Explore the Birmingham Negro Southern League Baseball Museum.

Exploring the Birmingham Negro Southern League (NSL) Baseball Museum is a journey into the rich history and cultural significance of African American baseball during the era of segregation. As you enter the museum, located in the historic district of Birmingham, you step into a world that celebrates the talent, resilience, and impact of African American baseball players.

Start your visit by immersing yourself in the exhibits that chronicle the history of the Negro Southern League. Learn about the formation of the league, its teams, players, and the challenges they faced in the face of racial segregation. The museum's displays, artifacts, and multimedia presentations provide a comprehensive narrative, shedding light on the often-overlooked contributions of African American athletes to the sport.

Take time to appreciate the memorabilia, photographs, and stories of legendary players who were integral to the Negro Southern League. The museum's commitment to preserving the legacy of these athletes ensures that their achievements are not forgotten, offering a platform for their stories to be told and celebrated.

Explore the interactive displays that allow you to engage with the history of the league. Test your knowledge of baseball trivia, discover the impact of the Negro Southern League on the broader civil rights movement, and gain insights into the resilience of players who persevered in the face of adversity.

As you navigate through the museum, pay special attention to the stories of Birmingham's own teams and players. The city played a significant role in the Negro Southern League, and the museum provides a localized perspective on the challenges and triumphs experienced by African American baseball communities in Birmingham.

Consider attending any special events, talks, or programs hosted by the museum. These offerings often provide a deeper understanding of the historical context and allow for a more immersive experience. Check the museum's schedule to see if there are any guided tours or educational sessions available during your visit.

Before leaving, explore the museum's gift shop, where you may find unique memorabilia, books, and souvenirs related to the Negro Southern League and African American baseball history. Purchasing items from the gift shop is a meaningful way to support the museum's ongoing efforts to preserve and share this vital aspect of sports history.

Visiting the Birmingham Negro Southern League Baseball Museum is not just a trip through baseball's past; it's an exploration of resilience, triumph over adversity, and the significant role that sports played in the fight for civil rights. It's a chance to honor the legacy of those who contributed to the Negro Southern League and to appreciate the enduring impact of African American athletes on the world of baseball.

# 37.Attend the Birmingham Art Crawl.

Attending the Birmingham Art Crawl is a dynamic and immersive experience that invites you to explore the city's vibrant artistic community, engage with local artists, and revel in the diverse expressions of creativity. As you make your way to the event, excitement builds for the artistic discoveries awaiting you in the heart of Birmingham.

The Birmingham Art Crawl typically transforms the city's streets into an open-air gallery, showcasing a wide array of artistic mediums, from paintings and sculptures to photography and mixed-media installations. Begin your journey by strolling through the designated areas, where local artists set up exhibits, creating a visually stimulating environment.

Interact directly with the artists, who are often present to share their inspiration, techniques, and personal stories behind their creations. This direct connection adds a personal touch to your experience, allowing you to gain insights into the local art scene and fostering a deeper appreciation for the creative process.

As you move from one exhibit to another, take note of the diversity in styles and themes presented by Birmingham's talented artists. The Birmingham Art Crawl embraces inclusivity, providing a platform for emerging and established artists alike, reflecting the city's rich cultural tapestry.

Explore nearby galleries, boutiques, and pop-up spaces that may participate in the art crawl, contributing to the overall artistic atmosphere. Many businesses collaborate with local artists to showcase their works, creating a symbiotic relationship between the arts community and the broader commercial landscape.

Enjoy live performances, music, or interactive art installations that are often part of the Birmingham Art Crawl. These elements add a dynamic and multisensory dimension to the event, creating a festive atmosphere and further emphasizing the city's commitment to fostering a vibrant cultural scene.

Consider engaging with fellow attendees, sharing your perspectives on the art on display, and perhaps even forming connections with other art enthusiasts. The Birmingham Art Crawl serves as a communal celebration of creativity, providing an opportunity for individuals from diverse backgrounds to come together and appreciate the transformative power of art.

Before concluding your visit, explore nearby cafes or restaurants that may be part of the art crawl route. Many establishments collaborate with the event, offering special promotions or creating an artsy ambiance that complements the overall experience.

Attending the Birmingham Art Crawl is not just about viewing art; it's about immersing yourself in the city's creative spirit, supporting local artists, and participating in a collective celebration of artistic expression. Whether you're a seasoned art connoisseur or someone discovering the joy of visual arts, the Birmingham Art Crawl promises a memorable and enriching experience in the heart of the city's cultural scene.

# 38.Go zip-lining at Red Mountain Park.

Embarking on a zip-lining adventure at Red Mountain Park is a thrilling and exhilarating experience that combines the beauty of nature with the excitement of high-flying adventure. As you arrive at Red Mountain Park, the anticipation builds for the breathtaking views and adrenaline-pumping moments that await.

Start your zip-lining journey by checking in at the park's adventure center. Here, you'll receive the necessary safety gear and a comprehensive briefing on the zip-lining course. The professional guides at Red Mountain Park prioritize safety, ensuring that participants are well-informed and equipped for the adventure ahead.

Hike to the zip-lining course, allowing you to immerse yourself in the natural beauty of Red Mountain Park. The park's lush forests, scenic trails, and panoramic views create a picturesque backdrop for your zip-lining adventure.

As you approach the launch platform, take a moment to absorb the stunning vistas that stretch out before you. Red Mountain Park offers a unique perspective of Birmingham, and the zip-lining course provides an exciting way to appreciate the landscape from a new angle.

Feel the adrenaline surge as you step off the platform and soar through the treetops. The rush of wind, the panoramic views, and the sensation of flying create an unforgettable experience. Red Mountain Park's zip-lining course typically consists of multiple lines, each varying in length and height, offering a series of thrilling descents.

Challenge yourself with different zip lines, each providing a unique perspective of the park's terrain. Whether you're a seasoned zip-liner or a first-time adventurer, the course caters to various skill levels, ensuring a memorable experience for everyone.

Take advantage of any guided tours or group experiences offered by Red Mountain Park. These options often enhance the adventure by providing additional insights into the park's ecology, history, and the significance of its conservation efforts.

Capture the moments by bringing a camera or using a helmet-mounted action camera if allowed. Documenting your zip-lining experience allows you to relive the excitement and share the adventure with friends and family.

After completing the zip-lining course, take a moment to celebrate your accomplishment and savor the sense of achievement. Consider exploring other recreational activities within Red Mountain Park, such as hiking trails or treetop adventures, to make the most of your visit.

Zip-lining at Red Mountain Park is not just an adrenaline rush; it's a chance to connect with nature, challenge yourself, and create lasting memories against the backdrop of Birmingham's scenic beauty. Whether you're an adventure enthusiast or someone seeking a unique outdoor experience, Red Mountain Park's zip-lining course promises an unforgettable journey through the treetops.

# 39. Visit the Arlington Antebellum Home and Gardens.

Visiting the Arlington Antebellum Home and Gardens is a step back in time, offering a glimpse into the Southern heritage and architectural elegance of the antebellum period. As you approach the estate, located in Birmingham, the grandeur of the antebellum home and the beauty of its gardens create an atmosphere of historic charm.

Begin your exploration with a guided tour of the Arlington mansion, an exquisite example of Greek Revival architecture. The knowledgeable guides provide insights into the history of the home, its original occupants, and the cultural context of the antebellum South. Admire the well-preserved period furnishings, elegant rooms, and architectural details that transport you to a bygone era.

Stroll through the meticulously maintained gardens that surround the mansion. The lush greenery, vibrant blooms, and carefully landscaped grounds reflect the beauty and serenity of Southern antebellum estates. Take your time to appreciate the historical significance of the gardens and the role they played in the daily life of those who once inhabited the property.

Explore the outbuildings on the estate, such as the original kitchen and slave quarters. These structures provide a sobering but essential perspective on the historical context of the antebellum South, offering insights into the lives of both the enslaved individuals and the affluent families who resided at Arlington.

Attend any special events or educational programs that may be hosted at Arlington Antebellum Home and Gardens. These events often delve deeper into various aspects of Southern history, architecture, or horticulture, providing an enriched experience for visitors seeking a more comprehensive understanding.

Capture the beauty of the estate by bringing a camera or smartphone. The well-preserved antebellum home and its surroundings offer picturesque settings, allowing you to document your visit and share the charm of Arlington with others.

Before concluding your visit, stop by the gift shop, where you may find souvenirs, books, and unique items related to the history and culture of the antebellum South. Supporting the gift shop contributes to the preservation efforts of Arlington Antebellum Home and Gardens.

Visiting Arlington is not just a tour of a historic home; it's an opportunity to appreciate the architectural legacy of the antebellum period, reflect on the complexities of Southern history, and immerse yourself in the beauty of carefully cultivated gardens. Whether you're a history enthusiast, a garden lover, or someone seeking a tranquil escape, Arlington Antebellum Home and Gardens offers a captivating journey into the past.

## 40. Take a food tour in the city.

Embarking on a food tour in Birmingham is a culinary adventure that allows you to savor the diverse and delicious flavors that define the city's vibrant food scene. As you set out on your food exploration, be prepared to indulge in a gastronomic journey that reflects Birmingham's rich culinary heritage and innovative dining culture.

Start your food tour by exploring the city's iconic neighborhoods, each known for its unique culinary offerings. Whether you're wandering through the historic districts or trendy urban areas, Birmingham's diverse culinary landscape ensures a range of delectable experiences.

Begin with a classic Southern breakfast at one of Birmingham's renowned breakfast spots. Indulge in fluffy biscuits, savory grits, and perhaps a serving of chicken and waffles. Many local establishments take pride in serving traditional Southern breakfasts with a modern twist.

For lunch, dive into Birmingham's barbecue scene. The city is known for its mouthwatering barbecue joints, where you can feast on slow-cooked ribs, pulled pork sandwiches, and a variety of flavorful sauces. Each barbecue spot has its own unique style, contributing to the rich tapestry of Birmingham's culinary identity.

Explore the city's diverse international cuisine for dinner. Birmingham's culinary scene embraces flavors from around the world, offering options ranging from authentic ethnic eateries to modern fusion restaurants. Sample dishes from local favorites, whether it's Mediterranean, Asian, Latin American, or other global influences.

Don't forget to indulge your sweet tooth with Birmingham's dessert offerings. From artisanal ice cream parlors to bakeries serving Southern-inspired treats, there are plenty of options to satisfy your cravings for something sweet.

Consider including a visit to one of Birmingham's bustling food markets or food truck gatherings. These venues showcase a variety of local vendors and provide an opportunity to taste a wide array of Birmingham's culinary delights in one location.

Throughout your food tour, engage with local chefs, restaurateurs, and fellow food enthusiasts. Birmingham's culinary community is passionate about sharing their creations and the stories behind them, adding a personal touch to your dining experiences.

As you traverse the city on your food tour, take in the ambiance of each dining establishment, from cozy cafes to upscale restaurants. The atmosphere contributes to the overall dining experience, providing a well-rounded exploration of Birmingham's gastronomic offerings.

Complete your food tour with a nightcap at one of Birmingham's craft breweries or cocktail bars. The city's beverage scene complements its culinary prowess, offering a variety of locally brewed beers, craft cocktails, and artisanal beverages.

Embarking on a food tour in Birmingham is not just about tasting delicious dishes; it's a journey into the heart of the city's culture, community, and creativity. Whether you're a dedicated foodie or someone looking to savor the flavors of Birmingham, a food tour promises a memorable and palate-pleasing experience.

# 41. Attend a Birmingham Bulls hockey game.

Attending a Birmingham Bulls hockey game is an exciting and spirited experience that immerses you in the thrilling world of ice hockey while embracing the vibrant sports culture of the city. As you make your way to the arena, anticipation builds for the fast-paced action and energetic atmosphere that awaits you.

Arrive early to soak in the pre-game excitement outside the venue. Engage with fellow fans, enjoy the camaraderie, and perhaps partake in the festivities that often accompany hockey games, such as tailgating or fan-driven events. The sense of community among Birmingham Bulls fans adds an extra layer of excitement to the overall game-day experience.

Enter the arena and feel the energy as you find your seat. The sound of skates slicing across the ice, the roar of the crowd, and the anticipation of the game about to unfold create an electric atmosphere. The Birmingham Bulls, a proud member of the Southern Professional Hockey League (SPHL), showcase top-notch talent, providing an exhilarating display of skill and sportsmanship.

Immerse yourself in the traditions of a hockey game, from the thrilling sound of the puck hitting the boards to the dramatic moments when players score goals. The fast-paced nature of hockey ensures that every second counts, keeping you on the edge of your seat throughout the game.

Participate in the cheers and chants of the crowd, adding your voice to the symphony of support for the Birmingham Bulls. The enthusiasm of fans contributes to the lively ambiance, creating an unforgettable sense of unity and pride in cheering for the home team.

Take advantage of the breaks between periods to explore the arena, visit the concession stands for classic game-time snacks, and perhaps pick up some team merchandise to commemorate your experience. Many hockey arenas also feature entertainment and activities to keep fans engaged during intermissions.

Capture the memorable moments by bringing a camera or smartphone. Document the excitement of the game, the passionate fan base, and any special events or promotions happening during your visit.

Whether you're a die-hard hockey fan or a newcomer to the sport, attending a Birmingham Bulls game is not just about watching a game; it's about being part of a dynamic community, embracing the competitive spirit, and celebrating the joy of live sports. The Birmingham Bulls provide a thrilling and entertaining experience that reflects the city's sports culture and fosters a sense of pride among its fans.

# 42. Explore the Birmingham Oddities and Curiosities Market.

Exploring the Birmingham Oddities and Curiosities Market is a fascinating and eclectic journey into the world of unique and unconventional treasures. As you step into the market, located in the heart of Birmingham, be prepared to encounter a diverse array of oddities, curiosities, and one-of-a-kind finds that showcase the city's vibrant and creative subcultures.

Begin your exploration by wandering through the market's stalls and exhibits. The vendors, each with their own distinctive collections, offer a captivating assortment of peculiar artifacts, vintage oddities, and curios that range from the whimsical to the macabre. From taxidermy and vintage medical equipment to unusual art pieces, the market is a treasure trove for those seeking the extraordinary.

Engage with the vendors and creators, as many are passionate collectors or artists eager to share the stories behind their unique items. The Birmingham Oddities and Curiosities Market often attracts a community of like-minded individuals, fostering an atmosphere of curiosity, creativity, and appreciation for the unusual.

Take your time to peruse the various sections of the market, each offering a different theme or category of curiosities. Whether you're interested in vintage oddities, alternative art, or offbeat collectibles, the market caters to a diverse range of tastes and interests.

Immerse yourself in the immersive and sometimes whimsical atmosphere created by the market organizers. Many oddities markets feature live performances, interactive installations, and themed decorations that add an extra layer of intrigue to the overall experience.

Consider attending any workshops, talks, or demonstrations that may be part of the market's programming. These sessions often provide insights into the history of certain oddities, artistic techniques, or the broader cultural significance of collecting and appreciating unconventional items.

Capture the uniqueness of the market by bringing a camera or smartphone. Document the peculiar and interesting discoveries you encounter, creating lasting memories of your visit to the Birmingham Oddities and Curiosities Market.

Before leaving, explore the surrounding area for any quirky or offbeat attractions that may complement your oddities market experience. Birmingham's alternative and artistic scenes often extend beyond the market venue, offering additional opportunities for exploration.

Participating in the Birmingham Oddities and Curiosities Market is not just about acquiring peculiar items; it's about embracing the unconventional, celebrating creativity, and connecting with a community that revels in the extraordinary. Whether you're a seasoned collector or simply curious, the market promises an unforgettable and delightfully eccentric adventure in the heart of Birmingham's subcultural landscape.

# 43.Attend the Fiesta Birmingham Latino Festival.

Attending the Fiesta Birmingham Latino Festival is a vibrant and culturally enriching experience that immerses you in the dynamic traditions, flavors, and festivities of the Latino community in Birmingham. As you join the celebration, located in the heart of the city, be prepared for a lively atmosphere filled with music, dance, delicious cuisine, and a strong sense of community.

Begin your Fiesta experience by exploring the diverse array of food vendors offering authentic Latino cuisine. From tacos and tamales to empanadas and paella, the festival showcases a rich tapestry of flavors that represent various Latin American countries. Indulge in the delicious dishes, savoring the spices and culinary traditions that make Latino cuisine so distinct and beloved.

Immerse yourself in the rhythmic beats and melodies of live music and dance performances. The Fiesta often features a lineup of talented musicians and dance groups representing different Latin American genres, creating an energetic and celebratory ambiance. Whether you're drawn to the passionate rhythms of salsa, the lively beats of cumbia, or the traditional sounds of mariachi, the festival provides a diverse musical experience.

Engage with the vibrant arts and crafts market, where local artisans showcase their talents through handmade goods, jewelry, and traditional crafts. This is an excellent opportunity to support local artists and take home unique, culturally significant souvenirs.

Participate in cultural workshops, demonstrations, or activities that may be offered during the festival. These sessions often provide insights into various aspects of Latino culture, from traditional dance steps to art techniques, fostering a deeper understanding of the rich heritage showcased at Fiesta.

Bring the whole family, as the Fiesta Birmingham Latino Festival typically offers a variety of family-friendly activities, including games, face painting, and entertainment for children. The inclusive nature of the festival ensures that attendees of all ages can enjoy the festivities.

Capture the colorful moments by bringing a camera or smartphone. Document the vibrant costumes, lively performances, and the overall joyous atmosphere of the Fiesta, creating lasting memories of your cultural celebration.

Before leaving, take a moment to connect with fellow festivalgoers and learn more about the diverse Latino community in Birmingham. The Fiesta serves as a platform for cultural exchange and understanding, promoting unity and appreciation for the rich traditions that contribute to the city's cultural tapestry.

Attending the Fiesta Birmingham Latino Festival is not just about experiencing a cultural celebration; it's about fostering community, embracing diversity, and reveling in the shared joy of music, dance, and cuisine. Whether you have Latin American roots or simply want to immerse yourself in a vibrant cultural experience, the Fiesta promises a lively and memorable celebration in the heart of Birmingham.

# 44. Take a paddleboat ride at Railroad Park.

Embarking on a paddleboat ride at Railroad Park is a serene and leisurely way to enjoy the outdoors while taking in the scenic beauty of this urban oasis in Birmingham. As you make your way to the park, located in the heart of the city, prepare for a relaxing experience surrounded by nature, water features, and the vibrant atmosphere of Birmingham's Railroad Park.

Start your paddleboat adventure by renting one of the charming paddleboats available at the park. The paddleboats often come in various designs, from traditional boats to whimsical swan or duck-shaped vessels. Choose the one that suits your preference and adds a touch of fun to your outing.

Navigate the serene waters of Railroad Park's picturesque lake, enjoying the tranquility and the lush greenery that surrounds you. The lake is a central feature of the park, providing a peaceful respite from the urban hustle and bustle. Paddle at your own pace, taking in the scenic views of the park, the skyline of Birmingham, and the architectural beauty that graces the waterfront.

Consider bringing along a friend or family member to share the experience. Paddleboats often accommodate multiple passengers, making it a social and enjoyable activity. The shared paddling experience adds a sense of camaraderie and allows you to appreciate the beauty of Railroad Park together.

Take advantage of the opportunity to spot local wildlife. The park's lake is home to ducks, geese, and other waterfowl, creating a delightful natural backdrop as you paddle. Keep an eye out for the peaceful coexistence of nature and urban life within the park.

Capture the scenic moments by bringing a camera or smartphone. Document your paddleboat ride, capturing the reflections on the water, the surrounding greenery, and the unique perspectives of Birmingham's skyline. These photos serve as mementos of your tranquil escape in the heart of the city.

After your paddleboat ride, explore other features of Railroad Park, such as walking trails, gardens, or the various events and activities that may be taking place. The park often hosts community events, concerts, and festivals, providing additional opportunities to enjoy the vibrant atmosphere.

Whether you're seeking a peaceful retreat, a romantic outing, or a family-friendly activity, a paddleboat ride at Railroad Park offers a delightful escape into nature within the urban landscape of Birmingham. It's a chance to unwind, appreciate the beauty of the surroundings, and create cherished memories in one of the city's most beloved green spaces.

# 45.Attend the Alabama Ballet performance.

Attending an Alabama Ballet performance is a captivating and culturally enriching experience that allows you to immerse yourself in the world of dance and artistic expression. As you anticipate the performance, held in Birmingham, prepare for an evening of elegance, grace, and the breathtaking movements of talented dancers.

Arrive at the venue with anticipation, ready to witness the artistry and precision of the Alabama Ballet. The company is known for its commitment to excellence in ballet, and the performances often showcase a diverse repertoire that includes classical ballets, contemporary works, and innovative choreography.

Take a moment to appreciate the ambiance of the theater as you find your seat. The Alabama Ballet performances are held in venues that contribute to the overall experience, providing a refined setting for the beauty and sophistication of the ballet.

As the performance begins, let the enchanting music, intricate choreography, and expressive storytelling transport you into the world of each ballet. Whether it's a timeless classic like "Swan Lake" or a modern piece pushing the boundaries of dance, the Alabama Ballet's performances are characterized by a commitment to artistic excellence and emotional resonance.

Marvel at the skill and athleticism of the dancers as they bring each piece to life. The Alabama Ballet attracts world-class talent, and the precision, strength, and artistry displayed on stage are a testament to the dedication of the performers and the artistic direction of the company.

Engage with the emotions evoked by the ballet, as each performance is a narrative told through movement. Whether it's a tale of love, tragedy, or the celebration of human expression, the Alabama Ballet excels in conveying stories through the universal language of dance.

Consider attending any pre-show talks, post-show discussions, or behind-the-scenes events that may be offered by the Alabama Ballet. These opportunities provide deeper insights into the creative process, the history of the ballets performed, and the dedication required to excel in the world of professional dance.

Capture the beauty of the performance by refraining from flash photography but feel free to take discreet photos during curtain calls or at designated times. Documenting the experience allows you to relive the magic of the ballet and share the artistic brilliance with others.

Before or after the performance, take a moment to explore the cultural scene surrounding the venue. Many theaters are located in areas that offer opportunities for fine dining, art galleries, or other cultural attractions, enhancing the overall experience of your evening with the Alabama Ballet.

Attending an Alabama Ballet performance is not just about watching dance; it's about connecting with the emotion, artistry, and sheer beauty of the ballet. Whether you're a seasoned ballet enthusiast or someone attending for the first time, the Alabama Ballet promises an enchanting and memorable journey into the world of dance and artistic expression.

## 46. Explore the Birmingham Fire Museum.

Exploring the Birmingham Fire Museum is a fascinating and educational journey that takes you through the history of firefighting and showcases the bravery and dedication of the men and women who have served in the Birmingham Fire and Rescue Service. Located in Birmingham, this museum provides a unique opportunity to learn about the evolution of firefighting techniques and equipment.

Begin your visit by immersing yourself in the exhibits that trace the history of the Birmingham Fire and Rescue Service. From the early days of hand-drawn fire engines to the modern firefighting equipment used today, the museum offers a comprehensive look at the advancements in technology and the challenges faced by firefighters over the years.

Marvel at the collection of vintage fire trucks and equipment on display. The Birmingham Fire Museum often features a variety of well-preserved apparatus, including historic fire engines, hoses, helmets, and other firefighting gear. The museum's exhibits provide a tangible connection to the past, allowing visitors to appreciate the craftsmanship and ingenuity of firefighting equipment through different eras.

Explore the interactive displays that offer insights into the daily lives of firefighters. Learn about the rigorous training, the camaraderie among fire crews, and the evolution of firefighting tactics. Many exhibits incorporate multimedia elements, such as photos, videos, and oral histories, enhancing the overall experience and providing a deeper understanding of the challenges faced by firefighters.

Engage with any hands-on activities or demonstrations that may be offered at the museum. These interactive elements provide a fun and educational experience, especially for younger visitors who can try on firefighting gear or participate in simulated rescue scenarios.

Take a moment to reflect on the historical significance of the Birmingham Fire and Rescue Service. The museum often pays tribute to firefighters who have served the community with dedication and valor. Memorials and displays honoring fallen heroes contribute to the museum's mission of preserving the legacy of those who have made sacrifices in the line of duty.

Consider joining a guided tour if available, as knowledgeable guides can provide additional context, anecdotes, and behind-the-scenes stories related to the exhibits. Their insights can deepen your appreciation for the history and impact of the Birmingham Fire and Rescue Service.

Before leaving, visit the museum's gift shop, where you may find firefighting-themed souvenirs, books, and memorabilia. Purchasing items from the gift shop supports the museum's ongoing efforts to preserve and share the history of firefighting in Birmingham.

Exploring the Birmingham Fire Museum is not just an educational experience; it's a tribute to the bravery and service of firefighters who have played a vital role in ensuring the safety of the community. Whether you have a personal connection to firefighting or simply want to gain a greater understanding of this essential profession, the museum offers a compelling and enlightening visit in the heart of Birmingham.

# 47.Take a scenic drive along the Shades Crest Road.

Embarking on a scenic drive along Shades Crest Road is a delightful and visually captivating journey that offers panoramic views of Birmingham and its picturesque surroundings. As you navigate this scenic route, located along the ridge of Shades Mountain, be prepared for breathtaking vistas, charming neighborhoods, and a tranquil escape within the city.

Begin your drive at an opportune time, such as late afternoon or early evening, to take advantage of the soft, golden hues of the setting sun. Shades Crest Road provides an excellent vantage point for enjoying sunset views over Birmingham, casting a warm glow on the landscape.

As you ascend along Shades Crest Road, savor the changing perspectives of the cityscape below. The road winds through residential neighborhoods, providing glimpses of charming homes, lush greenery, and the rolling hills that characterize this part of Birmingham.

Pause at the designated overlooks along the route to fully appreciate the expansive views. The overlooks offer platforms where you can stop, take a breath, and soak in the beauty of the surrounding landscape. Capture the scenic moments with a camera or simply enjoy the serenity of the elevated vantage points.

Explore the quaint neighborhoods that flank Shades Crest Road. Some sections feature tree-lined streets, historic architecture, and a peaceful ambiance. Consider taking detours to discover hidden gems or unique landmarks that add to the charm of the area.

Admire the natural beauty that surrounds Shades Crest Road. The drive takes you through areas with dense tree canopies, creating a tunnel of foliage that adds to the scenic allure. In the fall, the changing colors of the leaves enhance the visual spectacle, providing a vibrant tapestry of autumn hues.

Consider bringing along a picnic or snacks to enjoy at one of the designated parks or overlook areas. This allows you to take a leisurely break, relishing the tranquility and beauty of the surroundings.

Continue your drive until you reach the southernmost point of Shades Crest Road, where the views extend beyond Birmingham, showcasing the rolling hills and valleys that characterize the Alabama landscape.

Before concluding your scenic drive, take a moment to appreciate the sense of serenity and relaxation that Shades Crest Road offers. Whether you're a local seeking a peaceful escape or a visitor discovering the beauty of Birmingham, this scenic drive provides a rejuvenating experience within the city limits.

Embarking on a scenic drive along Shades Crest Road is not just about the journey; it's a chance to connect with nature, enjoy breathtaking views, and experience the tranquil beauty that exists within the city of Birmingham. Whether you're seeking a romantic outing, a solo escape, or a family adventure, Shades Crest Road promises a scenic drive filled with charm and natural splendor.

# 48.Attend the Taste of 4th Avenue Jazz Festival.

Attending the Taste of 4th Avenue Jazz Festival is an immersive and culturally rich experience that celebrates the heritage of Birmingham's Historic 4th Avenue Business District through the vibrant sounds of jazz, delicious food, and a lively community atmosphere. As you participate in this festival, held in the heart of Birmingham, be prepared to indulge in the rhythmic melodies, culinary delights, and the energetic spirit of the 4th Avenue community.

Arrive at the festival ready to explore the diverse offerings of jazz performances from local and regional musicians. The Taste of 4th Avenue Jazz Festival typically features a lineup of talented jazz artists, spanning various styles and traditions. Whether you're a seasoned jazz enthusiast or a newcomer to the genre, the festival provides a welcoming space to enjoy the soulful tunes and dynamic performances.

Savor the culinary delights offered by local vendors and food trucks participating in the festival. The "Taste" in the festival's name is a nod to the delicious array of food options available. From soul food and barbecue to international flavors, the culinary offerings reflect the diversity and richness of Birmingham's food scene.

Engage with the community by exploring the vendor booths and exhibits. Many local businesses and organizations participate, showcasing their products, services, and contributions to the 4th Avenue district. This creates a lively marketplace atmosphere, allowing you to connect with the community and discover the unique offerings of Birmingham's historic district.

Join in the festivities and activities designed for all ages. The Taste of 4th Avenue Jazz Festival often includes family-friendly events, interactive exhibits, and entertainment options for children, making it a well-rounded experience for attendees of all ages.

Consider attending any workshops, talks, or panel discussions that may be part of the festival's programming. These sessions often delve deeper into the history of jazz, the significance of the 4th Avenue district, and the cultural contributions of the local community.

Capture the moments by bringing a camera or smartphone. Document the vibrant performances, the community interactions, and the overall atmosphere of the festival. Sharing your experiences through photos allows you to relive the celebration and share the spirit of the Taste of 4th Avenue Jazz Festival with others.

Before leaving, take a stroll through the Historic 4th Avenue Business District. The area is rich in history and significance, featuring landmarks, murals, and architectural gems that contribute to Birmingham's cultural tapestry.

Attending the Taste of 4th Avenue Jazz Festival is not just about enjoying music and food; it's a celebration of community, culture, and the enduring legacy of the

4th Avenue district. Whether you're a jazz aficionado, a food lover, or someone eager to experience the vibrant spirit of Birmingham, the festival promises a memorable and enriching celebration in the heart of the city.

# 49.Explore the Birmingham Food Truck Roundup.

Exploring the Birmingham Food Truck Roundup is a delightful and flavorful adventure that immerses you in the diverse and creative culinary scene on wheels. Held in various locations throughout Birmingham, the Food Truck Roundup brings together a collection of mobile eateries, each offering a unique and mouthwatering menu. Here's what to expect when you join the gastronomic festivities.

Arrive at the Food Truck Roundup with an appetite and a sense of culinary curiosity. The roundup typically features a variety of food trucks, each specializing in different cuisines, from gourmet sandwiches and tacos to international flavors and inventive desserts.

Peruse the lineup of food trucks, taking note of the diverse offerings and the creative menus that make each truck stand out. Many food trucks pride themselves on unique and bold flavor combinations, providing a culinary experience that goes beyond traditional dining.

Engage with the chefs and food truck operators to learn more about their specialties, ingredients, and the inspiration behind their dishes. The food truck community often values direct interaction with customers, allowing you to get insights into the passion and creativity that drive these mobile kitchens.

Sample a variety of dishes from different food trucks to create your own culinary adventure. Whether you're in the mood for savory or sweet, traditional or avant-garde, the Food Truck Roundup provides options for every palate. Consider sharing dishes with friends or family to maximize the tasting experience.

Take advantage of communal seating areas or bring a picnic blanket to create your own outdoor dining space. The casual and social atmosphere of the Food Truck Roundup encourages mingling, sharing foodie recommendations, and enjoying the camaraderie of fellow food enthusiasts.

Explore the live entertainment or activities that may accompany the Food Truck Roundup. Some events feature live music, art installations, or family-friendly activities, enhancing the overall experience and creating a festive atmosphere.

Capture the culinary moments by bringing a camera or smartphone. Document your favorite dishes, the vibrant food truck setups, and the overall ambiance of the roundup. Sharing your foodie experiences on social media allows you to join the larger conversation around Birmingham's dynamic food scene.

Before leaving, check out any dessert or beverage options offered by the food trucks. Many dessert trucks and beverage vendors participate in the roundup, providing the perfect sweet or refreshing conclusion to your culinary exploration.

Exploring the Birmingham Food Truck Roundup is not just about eating; it's a celebration of creativity, community, and the culinary talents of Birmingham's mobile kitchens. Whether you're a seasoned foodie or someone looking for a fun and flavorful outing, the Food Truck Roundup promises a tasty and memorable experience in the heart of Birmingham.

# 50.Attend the Do Dah Day Parade.

Attending the Do Dah Day Parade is a lively and festive experience that immerses you in the spirit of community, celebration, and a colorful array of festivities. As you join this iconic event in Birmingham, be prepared for a day filled with whimsical floats, live music, and a joyful procession of people and pets.

Arrive early to secure a prime viewing spot along the parade route. Do Dah Day typically kicks off with a vibrant and eclectic parade that winds its way through the streets of Birmingham. Find a spot that allows you to enjoy the lively atmosphere and catch all the action as participants, pets, and creatively decorated floats pass by.

Celebrate the unique and creative floats that make up the Do Dah Day Parade. From whimsical designs to humorous themes, the floats reflect the community's creativity and sense of humor. Many participants go all out with costumes, decorations, and entertaining performances, contributing to the festive and lighthearted atmosphere.

Engage with the community as you enjoy the parade. Do Dah Day is known for its inclusive and welcoming spirit, bringing together people of all ages, backgrounds, and pet enthusiasts. Strike up conversations with fellow spectators, share a laugh, and enjoy the sense of camaraderie that permeates the event.

Capture the lively moments by bringing a camera or smartphone. Document the colorful floats, the exuberant participants, and the overall festive atmosphere. The Do Dah Day Parade provides ample photo opportunities, from creatively costumed pets to the joyous expressions of the crowd.

Participate in the various activities and events that take place throughout the day. Do Dah Day often features live music performances, food vendors, arts and crafts exhibits, and pet-centric activities. Explore the festivities beyond the parade route, immersing yourself in the diverse range of offerings.

Celebrate the unique pet-centric theme of Do Dah Day. Many participants bring their pets to join in the festivities, and the parade often features a variety of animals, from dogs and cats to more exotic pets. Enjoy the pet costume contests, agility demonstrations, and the heartwarming sight of pets and their owners celebrating together.

Before leaving, consider contributing to the charitable aspect of Do Dah Day. The event often serves as a fundraiser for local animal welfare organizations. Donations, merchandise purchases, or participation in fundraising activities help support these causes and contribute to the well-being of animals in the community.

Attending the Do Dah Day Parade is not just about watching a procession; it's a chance to immerse yourself in the joyous spirit of community, creativity, and the shared love for pets. Whether you're a pet owner, a parade enthusiast, or someone seeking a fun and festive outing, Do Dah Day promises a day filled with laughter, camaraderie, and the delight of a uniquely Birmingham celebration.

# 51. Take a historic tour of the Arlington House.

Embarking on a historic tour of Arlington House offers a fascinating journey into the past, allowing you to explore the rich history, architectural significance, and cultural heritage of this landmark in Birmingham. As you step into Arlington House, located in the historic Arlington Antebellum Home and Gardens, be prepared to immerse yourself in the stories and artifacts that have shaped this iconic residence.

Start your tour by taking in the exterior of Arlington House, appreciating its antebellum architecture and the well-preserved details that reflect the elegance of the era. The knowledgeable guides often provide an overview of the historical context, detailing the origins of the house and its role in Birmingham's history.

Enter the grand foyer and explore the various rooms that make up Arlington House. Each room is a window into the past, adorned with period-appropriate furnishings, decor, and artifacts. Learn about the architectural features, interior design choices, and the lifestyles of the families who once called Arlington House home.

Engage with the guided tour to gain insights into the social and cultural history associated with Arlington House. Guides often share stories about the original occupants, the challenges faced by the home's various owners, and the broader historical events that unfolded during the house's existence.

Visit the gardens surrounding Arlington House, which often reflect the charm and landscaping typical of the antebellum period. Stroll through the well-maintained grounds, appreciating the flora and design that contribute to the overall ambiance of the estate.

Learn about the restoration efforts that have preserved Arlington House and its historical significance. Many historic homes undergo meticulous restoration to ensure that they remain authentic to their original state, and guides may provide insights into the challenges and successes of preserving Arlington House for future generations.

Ask questions and engage with the guides to deepen your understanding of Arlington House and its place in Birmingham's history. Whether you're interested in architectural details, local lore, or the broader historical context, the guides are often eager to share their knowledge and foster a meaningful connection with visitors.

Capture the beauty and historical charm of Arlington House by bringing a camera or smartphone. Document the architectural details, period furnishings, and the serene surroundings to create lasting memories of your visit.

Before leaving, explore any additional exhibits, displays, or educational materials that may be available at Arlington House. Many historic homes have visitor centers or interpretive spaces that provide further context and enhance the overall learning experience.

Taking a historic tour of Arlington House is not just about exploring a physical structure; it's a journey through time, culture, and the stories that have shaped Birmingham's history. Whether you have a passion for architecture, a love of history, or simply enjoy immersing yourself in the past, Arlington House offers a captivating and educational experience within the heart of the city.

# 52. Attend the Birmingham International Street Fair.

Attending the Birmingham International Street Fair is an exciting and culturally enriching experience that brings together the diverse flavors, traditions, and entertainment from around the world. As you join this vibrant event in Birmingham, be prepared to immerse yourself in a global celebration featuring international cuisine, performances, and a lively atmosphere.

Arrive at the Birmingham International Street Fair with an open mind and a sense of curiosity. The fair typically showcases a diverse array of cultures, and each booth or section represents a different country or region. Explore the various offerings to discover new flavors, traditions, and artistry.

Savor the international cuisine available at the fair. From street food delicacies to traditional dishes, the Birmingham International Street Fair is a culinary journey around the globe. Enjoy the opportunity to try dishes from different countries, experiencing the rich tapestry of flavors that contribute to the global food scene.

Immerse yourself in the cultural performances and entertainment presented on the fair's stages. The event often features live music, dance performances, and traditional ceremonies representing the participating countries. Take a seat, enjoy the shows, and appreciate the diversity of talents showcased throughout the day.

Engage with the representatives at each booth to learn more about the cultural heritage, traditions, and customs of different countries. Many participants are enthusiastic about sharing insights into their cultures, offering a more immersive and educational experience for attendees.

Explore the arts and crafts exhibitions that may be part of the fair. Artisans often showcase traditional crafts, handmade goods, and cultural artifacts, providing an opportunity to purchase unique souvenirs and support international artists and creators.

Participate in any interactive activities or workshops that the fair may offer. From traditional dance lessons to language workshops, these hands-on experiences allow you to actively engage with the cultures being celebrated and gain a deeper understanding of their significance.

Capture the vibrant moments by bringing a camera or smartphone. Document the colorful displays, the energetic performances, and the overall festive atmosphere of the Birmingham International Street Fair. Sharing your experiences through photos allows you to celebrate the diversity and richness of the event.

Before leaving, check the event schedule for any special performances, parades, or ceremonies that may be happening later in the day. Some international fairs feature grand finales or processions that provide a memorable conclusion to the day's festivities.

Attending the Birmingham International Street Fair is not just about exploring different cultures; it's a celebration of diversity, unity, and the shared experiences that connect us all. Whether you're a seasoned traveler, a food enthusiast, or someone looking for a lively and inclusive event, the fair promises a dynamic and memorable celebration of global cultures in the heart of Birmingham.

# 53.Explore the Birmingham Historic Touring Company.

Exploring the Birmingham Historic Touring Company promises a fascinating journey through the city's rich history, guided by knowledgeable experts who share captivating stories, anecdotes, and insights. As you engage with the

Travel to Birmingham Alabama

Birmingham Historic Touring Company, be prepared to uncover the layers of history that have shaped Birmingham into the vibrant city it is today.

Start your exploration by checking the tour offerings provided by the Birmingham Historic Touring Company. Tours may cover a range of themes, from Civil Rights history and architectural landmarks to cultural districts and the industrial heritage of the city. Choose a tour that aligns with your interests to maximize your experience.

Join a guided walking tour or bus tour led by experienced and passionate guides. The Birmingham Historic Touring Company is likely to offer a variety of tour formats to accommodate different preferences and mobility levels. Whether you prefer strolling through historic districts on foot or comfortably exploring the city from a bus, the tours aim to provide an immersive and educational experience.

Engage with your guide to gain a deeper understanding of Birmingham's history, including key events, significant figures, and the evolution of the city over time. Guides often share intriguing anecdotes and little-known facts that add a personal and human touch to the historical narrative.

Visit iconic landmarks, historic neighborhoods, and cultural sites as part of the tour. The Birmingham Historic Touring Company aims to showcase the diversity and uniqueness of Birmingham's historical and cultural landscape. From the Civil Rights District to the industrial remnants of the city's past, each stop contributes to a comprehensive exploration of Birmingham's history.

Ask questions and participate in the dialogue during the tour. The guides are typically well-versed in Birmingham's history and are eager to foster an interactive and engaging experience. Take advantage of the opportunity to delve deeper into specific aspects of the city's history that intrigue you.

Capture the moments by bringing a camera or smartphone. Document the architectural gems, historical landmarks, and the overall atmosphere of the tour. Sharing your photos allows you to extend the experience and share the richness of Birmingham's history with others.

Consider custom or private tours if available. The Birmingham Historic Touring Company may offer personalized experiences tailored to specific interests or groups. Whether you're planning a private group outing or have specific historical topics you'd like to explore, custom tours provide a flexible and tailored approach.

Before concluding your exploration, check if the Birmingham Historic Touring Company offers any additional resources, such as books, maps, or recommended readings, to further enhance your understanding of Birmingham's history.

Exploring Birmingham with the Birmingham Historic Touring Company is not just about learning facts; it's a dynamic and immersive experience that connects you with the city's past. Whether you're a local resident or a visitor eager to delve into Birmingham's history, the tours offered by the Birmingham Historic Touring Company promise an enlightening and enriching journey through time.

# 54.Attend the Greater Birmingham Humane Society's Jazz Cat Ball.

Attending the Greater Birmingham Humane Society's Jazz Cat Ball is a delightful and philanthropic experience that combines the joy of jazz music with a celebration of compassion for animals. As you participate in this event, held in support of the Greater Birmingham Humane Society, be prepared for an evening filled with music, camaraderie, and a shared commitment to the well-being of animals.

Arrive at the Jazz Cat Ball dressed in your finest attire, as this event often features an elegant and festive atmosphere. The dress code may align with the theme of the evening, providing an opportunity to showcase your style while supporting a worthy cause.

Enjoy the musical performances that define the Jazz Cat Ball. Jazz music, with its soulful and vibrant tunes, sets the tone for the evening's festivities. Whether performed by live bands or featured on playlists, jazz adds a sophisticated and celebratory ambiance to the event.

Engage with fellow attendees who share a passion for animals and a commitment to supporting the Greater Birmingham Humane Society. The Jazz Cat Ball provides a social setting where you can connect with like-minded individuals, exchange stories, and enjoy the collective spirit of compassion for animals.

Participate in any fundraising activities or initiatives organized during the event. The Jazz Cat Ball often includes silent auctions, raffles, or donation opportunities to raise funds for the Greater Birmingham Humane Society's mission. Contributing to these efforts adds to the overall impact of the event and supports the organization's work in caring for animals in need.

Capture the memorable moments of the Jazz Cat Ball by bringing a camera or smartphone. Document the elegant decor, musical performances, and the joyous interactions among attendees. Sharing your experiences on social media can help raise awareness for the Greater Birmingham Humane Society and encourage others to support their cause.

Take part in any special activities or surprises that may be part of the Jazz Cat Ball. Some events include unique elements such as pet-friendly photo booths, interactive displays, or presentations that highlight the achievements and initiatives of the Greater Birmingham Humane Society.

Before leaving, express your support for the Greater Birmingham Humane Society by learning more about their programs, volunteering opportunities, and ways to stay involved beyond the Jazz Cat Ball. Many attendees find that the event becomes a gateway to ongoing engagement with the organization's mission.

Attending the Greater Birmingham Humane Society's Jazz Cat Ball is not just about enjoying a night of jazz and glamour; it's a meaningful way to contribute to the well-being of animals in the community. Whether you're an animal lover, a jazz enthusiast, or someone looking for a unique and philanthropic evening, the Jazz Cat Ball promises a memorable and impactful experience in support of a compassionate cause.

# 55.Take a cooking class in the city.

Embarking on a cooking class in the city is a delightful and hands-on experience that allows you to expand your culinary skills, discover new flavors, and connect with fellow food enthusiasts. As you participate in a cooking class, be prepared for a fun and educational journey through the world of gastronomy.

Choose a cooking class that aligns with your interests and preferences. Birmingham often offers a variety of classes covering diverse cuisines, cooking techniques, and skill levels. Whether you're a beginner or an experienced home cook, there's likely a class suited to your needs.

Arrive at the cooking class with an open mind and a willingness to learn. The instructors are typically experienced chefs or culinary experts who are passionate about sharing their knowledge. Take advantage of the opportunity to ask questions, seek advice, and absorb the culinary wisdom they impart.

Engage with your fellow participants, as cooking classes often foster a collaborative and social atmosphere. Share tips, exchange cooking experiences, and enjoy the camaraderie of working together in the kitchen. Cooking classes provide a unique opportunity to connect with others who share a love for food and cooking.

Follow the instructions and demonstrations provided by the instructor. Pay attention to the techniques, ingredients, and cooking tips shared during the class. Many instructors offer hands-on guidance, allowing you to practice and refine your skills under their expert supervision.

Experiment with new ingredients and flavors. Cooking classes often introduce participants to unique or unfamiliar ingredients, providing an opportunity to broaden your culinary horizons. Embrace the chance to taste, smell, and work with a diverse range of elements that contribute to the richness of the dishes being prepared.

Document the experience by taking notes and capturing photos of the dishes you create. Many cooking classes provide recipe cards or materials for you to reference later, allowing you to recreate the dishes at home. Documenting your culinary journey adds a personal touch to the experience and serves as a valuable reference for future cooking endeavors.

Enjoy the fruits of your labor by savoring the dishes you've prepared during the class. Whether it's a full-course meal or a selection of appetizers and desserts, relish the flavors and take pride in the culinary creations you've contributed to.

Before leaving, express gratitude to the instructor and fellow participants. Many cooking instructors appreciate feedback and enjoy hearing about your experience. Consider leaving a review or recommendation to help others discover the joys of the cooking class you attended.

Taking a cooking class in the city is not just about learning recipes; it's a dynamic and engaging experience that empowers you to become a more confident and skilled home cook. Whether you're seeking to enhance your culinary expertise, connect with others, or simply have a fun and educational outing, a cooking class in Birmingham promises a flavorful and rewarding adventure.

# 56.Explore the Freedom Walk at Kelly Ingram Park.

Exploring the Freedom Walk at Kelly Ingram Park is a moving and educational experience that takes you through a significant chapter in Birmingham's history, particularly during the Civil Rights Movement. As you traverse the Freedom Walk, located within Kelly Ingram Park, be prepared to immerse yourself in the poignant stories, sculptures, and landmarks that commemorate the struggle for civil rights.

Start your exploration at the entrance of Kelly Ingram Park, located in downtown Birmingham. The park itself is a serene and well-maintained space, but it holds profound historical significance as the site of numerous Civil Rights protests and events.

Engage with the sculptures and monuments that populate the park, each telling a unique story of the struggles and triumphs of the Civil Rights Movement. Notable sculptures include those by artist James Drake, such as the "Four Spirits" memorial, which commemorates the lives of the four girls tragically killed in the 16th Street Baptist Church bombing.

Walk along the Freedom Walk, which is a series of informational panels and exhibits providing a chronological narrative of the events that unfolded in Birmingham during the Civil Rights Movement. These exhibits guide you through the key moments, individuals, and protests that shaped the fight for equality.

Reflect at the "Letter From Birmingham Jail" display, which features excerpts from Martin Luther King Jr.'s powerful letter written during his time in the Birmingham Jail. The display provides insights into the moral and philosophical underpinnings of the Civil Rights Movement.

Pause at the "Foot Soldiers" sculpture, which depicts ordinary individuals who played extraordinary roles in the fight for civil rights. The depiction of men, women, and children in motion symbolizes the collective effort and determination of those who participated in the struggle.

Explore the "Path of Thorns and Roses," a pathway lined with inscriptions and sculptures that represent the hardships and triumphs experienced by Civil Rights activists. This symbolic journey invites contemplation on the sacrifices made in the pursuit of justice.

Take a moment to absorb the historical context of Kelly Ingram Park, recognizing that this space was once a focal point for protests, demonstrations, and clashes with law enforcement during the Civil Rights Movement. The park's transformation into a place of reflection and remembrance is a testament to the resilience and progress achieved.

Consider joining a guided tour of Kelly Ingram Park to gain deeper insights into the historical significance of each sculpture and exhibit. Knowledgeable guides often provide additional context, personal stories, and perspectives that enhance the overall experience.

Before leaving, visit the adjacent 16th Street Baptist Church, another pivotal site in the Civil Rights Movement. The church played a central role and was tragically targeted in the 1963 bombing that claimed the lives of four young girls.

Exploring the Freedom Walk at Kelly Ingram Park is not just a stroll through a tranquil green space; it's a journey through history, empathy, and the enduring pursuit of justice. Whether you're a history enthusiast, a seeker of social justice, or someone interested in understanding Birmingham's role in the Civil Rights Movement, the Freedom Walk offers a powerful and thought-provoking experience.

# 57.Attend the Alabama Asian Cultures and Food Festival.

Attending the Alabama Asian Cultures and Food Festival is a flavorful and culturally enriching experience that allows you to explore the diverse traditions, cuisines, and arts of the Asian continent. As you participate in this vibrant festival, be prepared for a day filled with delicious food, captivating performances, and a celebration of the rich cultural tapestry of Asia.

Arrive at the festival with an appetite and an open mind, as the Alabama Asian Cultures and Food Festival typically features a wide array of Asian cuisines. From traditional dishes to contemporary interpretations, you'll have the opportunity to savor the flavors of various countries and regions across Asia.

Explore the food stalls and vendors showcasing the culinary delights of Asia. Taste dishes from countries such as China, Japan, India, Vietnam, Korea, and more. Many vendors take pride in offering authentic and diverse options, allowing you to embark on a culinary journey through the diverse landscapes of Asian cuisine.

Engage with the cultural performances and exhibitions that take place throughout the festival. Traditional dance, music, martial arts demonstrations, and other artistic expressions provide a glimpse into the rich and diverse cultural heritage of Asian countries. Take a seat, enjoy the performances, and appreciate the talent and artistry on display.

Participate in interactive activities and workshops that may be part of the festival. From traditional crafts to language lessons, these hands-on experiences allow you to actively engage with Asian cultures and gain a deeper understanding of their traditions.

Explore the arts and crafts booths featuring handmade goods, traditional artifacts, and cultural displays. Many festivals include a marketplace where you can purchase unique items, textiles, and crafts from different Asian countries, providing an opportunity to take home a piece of the cultural richness you've experienced.

Capture the vibrant moments by bringing a camera or smartphone. Document the colorful displays, the energetic performances, and the overall festive atmosphere of the Alabama Asian Cultures and Food Festival. Sharing your experiences on social media allows you to celebrate the diversity and richness of Asian cultures with a broader audience.

Before leaving, consider attending any panel discussions or talks that may be part of the festival. These sessions often delve deeper into the cultural, historical, and social aspects of Asian countries, offering valuable insights and fostering a greater appreciation for the complexities of the region.

Attending the Alabama Asian Cultures and Food Festival is not just about enjoying delicious meals; it's a celebration of diversity, unity, and the shared experiences that connect us across continents. Whether you're a food enthusiast, a lover of the arts, or someone seeking a vibrant and inclusive cultural experience, the festival promises a day filled with discovery, appreciation, and celebration of the rich tapestry of Asian cultures.

# 58. Take a self-guided mural tour in Woodlawn.

Embarking on a self-guided mural tour in Woodlawn offers a visually captivating journey through this vibrant Birmingham neighborhood. As you explore the streets, alleys, and walls adorned with murals, be prepared to discover the creative expressions, stories, and artistic flair that contribute to the unique character of Woodlawn.

Start your mural tour by obtaining a map or a list of notable murals in Woodlawn. Local community centers, art organizations, or online resources may provide information on the locations of the murals and any additional context or background about the artists and their works.

Wander through the streets of Woodlawn with a keen eye for the colorful and dynamic murals that adorn the neighborhood. Murals often tell stories, convey messages, and reflect the cultural and social identity of the community. Take your time to appreciate the details, styles, and artistic techniques employed by the muralists.

Capture the beauty of the murals by bringing a camera or smartphone. Document your favorite pieces, interesting details, and the overall ambiance of the neighborhood. Many murals serve as public art, and sharing your photos on social media can contribute to the broader appreciation of Woodlawn's artistic landscape.

Engage with the community as you explore the murals. Woodlawn is known for its active and vibrant community, and you may encounter locals who can share insights into the significance of certain murals or provide additional recommendations for your tour.

Visit the Woodlawn Street Market or local cafes and businesses, as they often serve as hubs for community engagement and may feature murals on their exterior walls. These spaces can add an extra layer to your self-guided tour and provide opportunities to connect with the neighborhood's cultural scene.

Take note of any recurring themes, messages, or symbols that you observe across multiple murals. These elements can provide a deeper understanding of the shared narratives and values within the Woodlawn community.

Explore both well-known and hidden gems. While some murals may be widely recognized, others might be tucked away in less-trafficked areas. A sense of curiosity and a willingness to explore off the beaten path can lead to delightful discoveries.

Reflect on the impact of public art on community identity and cohesion. Consider how the murals contribute to the cultural richness of Woodlawn and serve as a form of storytelling and self-expression for both local artists and the community as a whole.

Before concluding your tour, take a moment to appreciate the collective effort that goes into maintaining and promoting public art in Woodlawn. Public art often involves collaboration between artists, community members, and local organizations, contributing to the vitality and pride of the neighborhood.

Embarking on a self-guided mural tour in Woodlawn is not just about viewing art on walls; it's a dynamic and immersive experience that allows you to connect with the community, explore the neighborhood's identity, and appreciate the power of public art in shaping the cultural landscape. Whether you're an art enthusiast, a local resident, or a visitor seeking a unique and visually stimulating adventure, Woodlawn's murals promise a rich and colorful journey.

# 59. Visit the Oak Hill Cemetery.

Visiting Oak Hill Cemetery is a contemplative and historically significant experience that offers a glimpse into Birmingham's past and the lives of its residents. As you explore this serene burial ground, be prepared to encounter unique monuments, historical markers, and a tranquil atmosphere that invites reflection.

Upon arriving at Oak Hill Cemetery, take a moment to appreciate the cemetery's historical significance. Established in the late 1800s, Oak Hill is the final resting place for many individuals who played key roles in Birmingham's development and history.

Explore the architectural and artistic elements of the gravestones and monuments. Oak Hill Cemetery features a variety of tombstones, markers, and memorials that reflect different styles and periods of cemetery art. Pay attention to the inscriptions, symbols, and designs, as they often provide insights into the individual's life and the cultural norms of the time.

Walk through the different sections of the cemetery, each with its own character and ambiance. Some areas may feature family plots, while others may highlight the final resting places of prominent figures in Birmingham's history. Stroll along the pathways and take in the peaceful surroundings.

Visit the gravesites of notable individuals interred at Oak Hill Cemetery. Some graves may belong to local leaders, pioneers, or historical figures who have left a lasting impact on the community. Historical markers or informational materials may provide additional context about these individuals and their contributions.

Pause at the Oak Hill Mausoleum if it is part of the cemetery. Mausoleums often showcase unique architecture and house the final resting places of multiple individuals. Take a moment of quiet reflection in these spaces.

Note any natural or landscaping features that enhance the cemetery's beauty. Oak Hill Cemetery is often designed with care to provide a serene and aesthetically pleasing environment. Trees, flowers, and well-maintained green spaces contribute to the overall tranquility of the site.

Consider the historical context of the cemetery and its role in preserving the memory of Birmingham's past. Cemeteries like Oak Hill serve as both a repository of local history and a place for quiet contemplation, providing a link between the present and the stories of those who came before.

Bring a camera or sketchbook to document the unique elements and scenes that capture your attention. Photography or sketching can be a thoughtful way to engage with the art, architecture, and atmosphere of Oak Hill Cemetery.

Respect the solemnity of the space and the privacy of those who may be visiting loved ones' graves. Keep noise levels low and be mindful of the peaceful environment.

Before leaving, consider checking if there are any guided tours or events scheduled at Oak Hill Cemetery. Some cemeteries offer tours that provide in-depth information about the history, architecture, and notable residents.

Visiting Oak Hill Cemetery is not just about acknowledging the inevitability of life; it's a thoughtful exploration of history, art, and the individuals who have shaped Birmingham. Whether you're interested in local history, genealogy, or seeking a place for quiet contemplation, Oak Hill Cemetery offers a poignant and enriching experience.

# 60.Attend a play at the Virginia Samford Theatre.

Attending a play at the Virginia Samford Theatre is a cultural and theatrical experience that promises an evening of entertainment, artistic expression, and a celebration of the performing arts. As you step into this historic venue, be prepared to immerse yourself in the world of live theater and enjoy a memorable performance.

Arrive at the Virginia Samford Theatre with anticipation and excitement. The venue, housed in a beautifully restored historic building, offers a charming and intimate setting for theatrical productions. Take in the architectural details and the ambiance that sets the stage for a captivating performance.

Check the schedule in advance to see what plays or productions are currently being featured. The Virginia Samford Theatre hosts a variety of performances, including classic plays, contemporary dramas, musicals, and more. Choose a show that aligns with your interests and preferences.

Secure your tickets ahead of time to ensure you have a seat for the performance. The Virginia Samford Theatre may offer online ticketing or box office options. Consider arriving early to explore the theater space and enjoy any pre-show activities or amenities.

Engage with the artistic community by checking if there are any pre-show discussions, talkbacks, or behind-the-scenes tours available. These opportunities provide additional insights into the production, the creative process, and the world of theater.

Take your seat in the theater and immerse yourself in the performance. Live theater offers a unique and dynamic experience, allowing you to connect with the actors, the story, and the emotions unfolding on stage. Be attentive to the nuances of the performances and appreciate the talent of the cast.

Capture the memories by refraining from flash photography during the performance but consider taking a photo of the theater or cast during curtain call if permitted. Share your experience on social media to encourage others to explore the vibrant arts scene in Birmingham.

Consider supporting the Virginia Samford Theatre by checking if there are opportunities for donations, memberships, or volunteering. Theatrical venues often rely on community support to continue providing quality productions and fostering a love for the arts.

After the play, take a moment to reflect on the performance. Discuss the production with fellow attendees, share your thoughts, and appreciate the impact of live theater on the cultural vibrancy of Birmingham.

If the Virginia Samford Theatre has a lobby or reception area, explore it after the show. Some venues feature artwork, exhibits, or spaces where you can continue to appreciate the arts in a more relaxed setting.

Attending a play at the Virginia Samford Theatre is not just about witnessing a performance; it's an opportunity to connect with the rich tradition of live theater, support the local arts community, and experience the magic of storytelling brought to life on stage. Whether you're a seasoned theatergoer or a first-time attendee, the Virginia Samford Theatre promises a delightful and engaging evening of theatrical entertainment.

# 61.Explore the Village Creek Greenway.

Exploring the Village Creek Greenway is a refreshing and nature-filled experience that allows you to connect with the outdoors, enjoy scenic views, and engage in recreational activities. As you embark on your journey along the greenway, be prepared to immerse yourself in the natural beauty and tranquility it offers.

Travel to Birmingham Alabama

Start your exploration by accessing the Village Creek Greenway at one of its entry points. The greenway is designed for walking, running, cycling, and other non-motorized activities, providing a welcoming space for outdoor enthusiasts of all ages.

Take a leisurely stroll or an invigorating jog along the well-maintained paths of the greenway. The trails wind through diverse landscapes, including wooded areas, open spaces, and waterfront sections along Village Creek. Pay attention to the sounds of nature and enjoy the serenity of the surroundings.

Bring a bicycle if you prefer cycling, as the greenway is often bike-friendly. Pedal at your own pace and explore the various segments of the trail system. Biking allows you to cover more ground while enjoying the fresh air and scenic views.

Pause at designated resting spots, benches, or scenic overlooks along the greenway. These areas provide opportunities to take in the natural beauty, observe wildlife, and even enjoy a picnic if you bring snacks or a packed lunch.

Explore the waterfront sections of the Village Creek Greenway. Depending on the trail, you may encounter serene creekside paths, footbridges, or areas where you can enjoy views of Village Creek. Water features add an extra layer of tranquility to the overall experience.

Capture the beauty of the natural surroundings by bringing a camera or smartphone. Document the lush greenery, picturesque landscapes, and any wildlife you encounter. Photography is a wonderful way to preserve the memories of your outdoor adventure.

Consider bringing binoculars if you're interested in birdwatching. The Village Creek Greenway is often home to a variety of bird species, providing birdwatchers with opportunities to observe and identify different feathered residents.

Check if there are any organized events or community activities taking place along the greenway. Some areas may host nature walks, educational programs, or environmental initiatives. Participating in these events can enhance your understanding of the local ecosystem and community engagement.

Respect the natural environment by adhering to Leave No Trace principles. Dispose of any waste properly, stay on designated trails, and avoid disturbing wildlife. Responsible exploration ensures the preservation of the greenway for future generations.

Before concluding your adventure, take a moment to appreciate the benefits of spending time in nature. Whether you seek solitude, exercise, or simply a break from the urban environment, the Village Creek Greenway offers a peaceful retreat where you can recharge and connect with the outdoors.

Exploring the Village Creek Greenway is not just about walking a trail; it's a holistic experience that invites you to appreciate the beauty of nature, engage in outdoor activities, and foster a sense of well-being. Whether you're a nature enthusiast, a fitness seeker, or someone looking for a peaceful escape, the greenway provides a welcoming and rejuvenating environment.

# 62. Attend the Birmingham Ethnic Festival.

Attending the Birmingham Ethnic Festival is a cultural and festive experience that celebrates the rich diversity of Birmingham's community. As you participate in this vibrant event, be prepared for a day filled with cultural performances, delicious international cuisine, and a lively atmosphere that showcases the city's multicultural spirit.

Arrive at the Birmingham Ethnic Festival with an open mind and a sense of curiosity. This event typically features a diverse array of cultures, traditions, and ethnicities coming together to share their heritage. Take in the sights, sounds, and aromas that reflect the global tapestry of Birmingham.

Explore the different cultural booths and exhibits showcasing the traditions, clothing, and artifacts of various ethnic groups. Engage with the community members who are eager to share their heritage and educate visitors about the cultural richness they represent.

Indulge in the culinary delights offered by the diverse food vendors. From traditional dishes to international flavors, the Birmingham Ethnic Festival is a culinary journey that allows you to savor a wide range of delicious foods. Consider trying dishes from different cultures to expand your palate and experience the global culinary offerings.

Enjoy the cultural performances and entertainment on the festival's stages. Traditional music, dance, and performances often take center stage, providing a dynamic and engaging experience. Participate in any dance workshops, cultural demonstrations, or interactive activities that may be part of the festival's program.

Visit the arts and crafts booths featuring handmade goods, traditional artworks, and cultural souvenirs. Support local artisans and take home unique items that reflect the craftsmanship and artistic expressions of different cultures.

Capture the lively moments of the festival by bringing a camera or smartphone. Document the colorful performances, the diverse crowd, and the overall festive atmosphere. Sharing your experiences on social media can contribute to the celebration of Birmingham's cultural diversity.

Engage in conversations with fellow attendees and participants. The Birmingham Ethnic Festival is an opportunity to connect with people from various backgrounds, exchange stories, and appreciate the shared values that unite the community.

Check if there are any cultural parades or processions scheduled as part of the festival. Parades often feature vibrant costumes, music, and dance, adding an extra layer of excitement to the event.

Before leaving, express gratitude to the organizers, volunteers, and participants who contribute to the success of the Birmingham Ethnic Festival. Consider leaving feedback or testimonials to show your appreciation for the efforts that go into creating this cultural celebration.

Attending the Birmingham Ethnic Festival is not just about experiencing different cultures; it's a celebration of unity, diversity, and the collective strength that comes from embracing various backgrounds. Whether you're a Birmingham resident, a visitor, or someone eager to explore the multicultural facets of the city, the Birmingham Ethnic Festival promises a day of cultural enrichment and community celebration.

# 63. Take a scenic drive on Highway 280.

Embarking on a scenic drive on Highway 280 is a picturesque journey that offers stunning landscapes, charming towns, and the allure of Alabama's natural beauty. As you travel along this route, be prepared for a visually appealing adventure and the opportunity to discover the scenic wonders along the way.

Start your scenic drive on Highway 280 with a full tank of gas and a sense of wanderlust. This highway meanders through diverse landscapes, providing a mix of rural and suburban scenery as well as glimpses of Alabama's countryside.

Enjoy the scenic views as you drive through rolling hills and open fields. Highway 280 is known for its picturesque landscapes, especially as you approach the Birmingham area. Take in the natural beauty and the changing colors of the seasons, from lush greenery to vibrant autumn foliage.

Consider making stops at scenic overlooks or designated pull-off areas along the highway. These spots often provide panoramic views of the surrounding countryside, allowing you to capture the beauty of the landscape with a camera or simply soak in the tranquility.

Explore charming towns and communities along the route. Highway 280 passes through areas with unique character and local charm. Consider detouring into towns such as Chelsea, Sylacauga, or Alexander City to experience local culture, shops, and dining options.

Appreciate the small-town charm of communities along the way, from roadside markets to historic landmarks. Each town along Highway 280 has its own story to tell, contributing to the overall richness of the journey.

Keep an eye out for points of interest or attractions along the route. Depending on your interests, you may encounter parks, lakes, or cultural sites that are worth exploring. These detours can add a layer of discovery to your scenic drive.

Drive at a leisurely pace to fully appreciate the surroundings and take in the scenic beauty. Highway 280 offers a balance of peaceful stretches and more lively areas, allowing you to tailor your driving experience to your preferences.

Bring along snacks, beverages, and a road map to enhance your journey. Having refreshments on hand and a map to guide you can make the drive more enjoyable, allowing you to stop at scenic spots or plan detours based on your interests.

Capture the moments with photos or simply enjoy the ride without any particular destination in mind. Whether you're a photography enthusiast or someone seeking a peaceful drive, Highway 280 provides ample opportunities for both.

Before concluding your scenic drive, take a moment to reflect on the beauty of the journey and the diverse landscapes you've encountered. Whether you've driven a short segment or the full length of Highway 280, the experience offers a memorable exploration of Alabama's scenic wonders.

# 64.Explore the Ensley SoHo neighborhood.

Exploring the Ensley SoHo neighborhood is a journey through history, culture, and community in Birmingham. As you navigate this unique area, be prepared to encounter a blend of historic architecture, vibrant street art, and local businesses that contribute to the neighborhood's distinctive character.

Start your exploration of the Ensley SoHo neighborhood by wandering through its streets and taking in the architectural charm. Ensley is known for its historic buildings, some dating back to the early 20th century when the area thrived as an industrial and commercial hub. Notice the unique details and craftsmanship that showcase the neighborhood's rich history.

Discover the vibrant street art that adorns some of the buildings and walls in Ensley. Street murals often reflect the spirit of the community and contribute to the artistic ambiance of the neighborhood. Take your time to appreciate the creativity and expressions of local artists.

Visit local businesses and shops to get a sense of the neighborhood's current energy and the entrepreneurial spirit of its residents. Ensley SoHo is home to a variety of establishments, including cafes, boutiques, and art galleries. Engage with the locals, explore their offerings, and support the community's economic growth.

Explore the Ensley Historic District, which is listed on the National Register of Historic Places. This district showcases the architectural legacy of Ensley and provides insights into its industrial past. The district includes notable structures such as the Ramsay-McCormack Building and the TCI Company Store, offering a glimpse into the neighborhood's history.

Take a stroll through SoHo Square, a public space that serves as a gathering point for community events and activities. Whether it's a local market, cultural celebration, or outdoor performance, SoHo Square often hosts events that bring residents together. Check local event listings to see if there are any happenings during your visit.

Dine at local restaurants and cafes to experience the culinary offerings of Ensley SoHo. Many establishments in the area showcase a mix of traditional and contemporary flavors, contributing to the neighborhood's gastronomic diversity. Engage with the local culinary scene and savor the unique tastes that reflect the community's cultural influences.

Attend community events or festivals that may be taking place in Ensley SoHo. These gatherings often provide opportunities to connect with residents, learn more about local initiatives, and participate in the neighborhood's vibrant social fabric.

Learn about community initiatives or revitalization efforts that are underway in Ensley SoHo. The neighborhood has seen various revitalization projects aimed at preserving its history while fostering economic and cultural growth. Consider engaging with local organizations or community groups to gain insights into ongoing developments.

Before concluding your exploration, take a moment to appreciate the resilience and sense of community that defines Ensley SoHo. Whether you're fascinated by its history, inspired by its artistic expressions, or simply drawn to the warmth of its residents, the neighborhood offers a unique and authentic experience that reflects the dynamic spirit of Birmingham.

# 65.Attend a film screening at the Birmingham Public Library.

Attending a film screening at the Birmingham Public Library is a cultural and cinematic experience that combines the love of movies with the community-oriented atmosphere of a public library. As you step into this literary and cinematic hub, be prepared for an enriching event that may include diverse films, insightful discussions, and a celebration of storytelling through the visual medium.

Check the Birmingham Public Library's event calendar or contact the library in advance to find information about upcoming film screenings. The library often hosts screenings of documentaries, classic films, independent productions, or movies that tie into specific themes or cultural events.

# Travel to Birmingham Alabama

Arrive at the library with enough time to explore the surroundings and get a feel for the cultural ambiance of the venue. Many libraries, including the Birmingham Public Library, strive to create welcoming spaces that foster community engagement.

Participate in any pre-screening discussions or activities that may be organized by the library. Some screenings include introductions, Q&A sessions, or panel discussions with filmmakers or experts, providing additional insights into the films and their themes.

Take your seat in the library's designated screening area and immerse yourself in the cinematic experience. Libraries often provide a comfortable and intimate setting for film screenings, allowing you to focus on the storytelling and visual elements of the movie.

Engage with fellow attendees by sharing your thoughts, reactions, and observations during and after the film. Film screenings at the library offer a communal experience, and discussions with other movie enthusiasts can enhance your understanding and appreciation of the films.

Consider bringing a notebook or electronic device to jot down any insights, reflections, or questions that arise during the screening. Libraries often encourage thoughtful engagement with the content, and your observations may contribute to post-screening discussions.

Explore the library's resources related to the films being screened. Public libraries frequently curate book collections, articles, or additional materials that complement the themes explored in the movies. Take advantage of the opportunity to delve deeper into the subjects that capture your interest.

Support the library's film programming by checking if there are any membership programs, donations, or ways to get involved in promoting film culture within the community. Many libraries rely on community support to continue offering diverse and engaging cultural events.

Before leaving, express appreciation to the library staff and organizers for their efforts in curating film screenings and fostering a cultural space within the community. Libraries play a vital role in promoting access to knowledge and culture, and your acknowledgment contributes to their mission.

Attending a film screening at the Birmingham Public Library is not just about watching movies; it's an opportunity to engage with cinematic art, connect with the community, and celebrate the library as a cultural hub. Whether you're a film enthusiast, a library supporter, or someone seeking a unique cultural experience, the library's film screenings promise an enjoyable and thought-provoking journey into the world of storytelling through film.

# 66. Take a yoga class at Railroad Park.

Embarking on a yoga class at Railroad Park offers a serene and revitalizing experience that combines the benefits of yoga practice with the natural beauty of this urban oasis. As you join the class in this picturesque setting, be prepared for a harmonious blend of mindfulness, physical well-being, and connection with nature.

Check the schedule for yoga classes at Railroad Park in advance. The park often hosts outdoor yoga sessions, especially during favorable weather conditions. Confirm the class details, including the time, location within the park, and any specific requirements for participants.

Arrive at Railroad Park a little early to find a suitable spot for your yoga practice. Whether it's on the grassy lawn, a designated yoga area, or any predetermined location, choose a space that allows you to fully immerse yourself in the experience.

Bring a yoga mat, water bottle, and any additional props you may need for your practice. Practicing yoga outdoors presents a unique opportunity to connect with the natural elements, so ensure you have everything necessary for a comfortable and focused session.

Take a moment to center yourself before the class begins. Embrace the tranquil surroundings of Railroad Park, appreciate the open sky above you, and tune in to the sounds of nature around you. This initial mindfulness can enhance the overall yoga experience.

Engage wholeheartedly in the yoga class led by the instructor. Follow the guidance, practice your poses, and be attuned to the rhythm of your breath. Outdoor yoga allows you to connect with the earth beneath you, fostering a sense of grounding and balance.

Appreciate the scenic views of Railroad Park during your yoga practice. The park's design, with its lake, walking trails, and green spaces, provides a serene backdrop for your movements. Allow yourself to be present in the moment and absorb the beauty of your surroundings.

Connect with fellow participants and the instructor during and after the class. Outdoor yoga sessions often cultivate a sense of community, and sharing the experience with others can add a social and supportive element to your practice.

Consider incorporating mindfulness or meditation into your practice. Take a few moments of stillness to absorb the positive energy of the park, listen to the sounds of nature, and cultivate a sense of inner peace.

Capture the experience by taking a photo or simply reveling in the post-yoga glow. Sharing your outdoor yoga journey on social media can inspire others to explore the benefits of practicing in natural settings.

Before leaving, express gratitude to the instructor and fellow participants. Thank the park staff for providing the opportunity to enjoy yoga in such a beautiful environment. Reflect on the sense of rejuvenation and well-being that outdoor yoga at Railroad Park has brought to your day.

Taking a yoga class at Railroad Park is not just about physical exercise; it's a holistic experience that integrates mindfulness, nature, and community. Whether you're a seasoned yogi or a beginner, practicing yoga in this urban oasis offers a unique and refreshing way to nurture your mind, body, and spirit.

# 67.Attend the Alabama Multicultural Street Fair.

Attending the Alabama Multicultural Street Fair is a vibrant and festive experience that celebrates the diverse cultures that contribute to the fabric of the state. As you immerse yourself in this dynamic event, be prepared for a lively atmosphere, cultural performances, delicious international cuisine, and a celebration of unity in diversity.

Arrive at the Alabama Multicultural Street Fair with an open mind and a spirit of curiosity. The fair typically showcases the traditions, customs, and artistry of various cultural communities, creating a rich tapestry of experiences for attendees.

Explore the different cultural booths and exhibits that highlight the heritage of participating communities. From traditional clothing and artifacts to informational displays, each booth offers a unique window into the cultural richness that makes up Alabama's multicultural landscape.

Indulge in the culinary delights offered by the diverse food vendors. The street fair is an opportunity to savor a wide array of international cuisines, from savory dishes to sweet treats. Consider trying dishes from cultures you may be less familiar with, expanding your culinary palate.

Enjoy the cultural performances on the fair's stages. Traditional music, dance, and other artistic expressions often take center stage, providing a dynamic and engaging experience. Take part in any dance workshops, cultural demonstrations, or interactive activities that may be part of the fair's program.

Participate in the interactive elements of the street fair. Some fairs feature hands-on activities, workshops, or demonstrations that allow attendees to actively engage with different aspects of various cultures. These activities provide a deeper understanding and appreciation of diversity.

Capture the lively and colorful moments of the fair by bringing a camera or smartphone. Document the vibrant performances, the diverse crowd, and the overall festive atmosphere. Sharing your experiences on social media can contribute to the celebration of multiculturalism.

Engage in conversations with fellow fairgoers and participants. The Alabama Multicultural Street Fair is a gathering place for people from various backgrounds, and interacting with others allows you to exchange stories, learn about different cultures, and celebrate the shared values that unite the community.

Check if there are any parades, processions, or cultural showcases scheduled as part of the fair. These events often feature vibrant costumes, music, and dance, adding an extra layer of excitement and spectacle to the celebration.

Before leaving, express gratitude to the organizers, volunteers, and participants who contribute to the success of the Alabama Multicultural Street Fair. Consider leaving feedback or testimonials to show your appreciation for the efforts that go into creating this cultural celebration.

Attending the Alabama Multicultural Street Fair is not just about witnessing cultural diversity; it's a celebration of unity, understanding, and the collective strength that comes from embracing various backgrounds. Whether you're a local resident, a visitor, or someone eager to explore the multicultural facets of Alabama, the street fair promises a day of cultural enrichment and community celebration.

# 68.Explore the Birmingham Black Barons Hall of Fame.

Exploring the Birmingham Black Barons Hall of Fame is a journey into the rich history of the Negro Leagues and the significant contributions of the Birmingham Black Barons to baseball. As you delve into this Hall of Fame, be prepared for an immersive experience that highlights the achievements, struggles, and legacy of this historic baseball team.

Upon entering the Birmingham Black Barons Hall of Fame, take a moment to appreciate the historical context. The Black Barons were a professional baseball team in the Negro Leagues, which operated during a time of racial segregation in the United States. Understand the importance of the Negro Leagues in providing opportunities for African American athletes who were excluded from Major League Baseball.

Explore the exhibits and displays that showcase the achievements of the Birmingham Black Barons. From team memorabilia and photographs to individual player profiles, the Hall of Fame offers a comprehensive overview of the team's history and the talented individuals who contributed to its success.

Learn about the iconic players who wore the Birmingham Black Barons uniform. Discover their stories, accomplishments, and the challenges they faced during an era of racial inequality in sports. The Hall of Fame provides a platform to celebrate the talent and resilience of these athletes.

Examine the artifacts and memorabilia that are part of the Hall of Fame's collection. This may include baseball equipment, uniforms, newspaper clippings, and other historical items that offer a tangible connection to the team's past. These artifacts provide a glimpse into the everyday lives and experiences of the players.

Take note of any interactive elements within the Hall of Fame. Some exhibits may include multimedia presentations, audio recordings, or interactive displays that enhance the visitor's understanding of the Birmingham Black Barons' legacy. Engage with these features to gain a deeper appreciation for the team's impact.

Consider the social and cultural significance of the Birmingham Black Barons in the broader context of American history. Reflect on how the team's success and challenges contributed to breaking down racial barriers and advancing the cause of civil rights.

Attend any guided tours or educational programs that may be offered at the Hall of Fame. Knowledgeable guides can provide additional insights, anecdotes, and context that enrich your understanding of the Birmingham Black Barons and the Negro Leagues.

Capture the experience by taking photographs of the exhibits and displays. Documenting your visit allows you to share the history of the Birmingham Black Barons with others and serves as a personal reminder of the impact of this historic baseball team.

Before leaving the Hall of Fame, consider browsing the gift shop if available. Many museums and Halls of Fame offer memorabilia, books, and souvenirs related to the exhibits, providing an opportunity to take home a piece of the history you've explored.

Exploring the Birmingham Black Barons Hall of Fame is not just about baseball; it's a tribute to the resilience, talent, and contributions of African American athletes during a challenging period in American history. Whether you're a baseball enthusiast, a history buff, or someone interested in the cultural impact of sports, the Hall of Fame offers a compelling and educational experience.

# 69. Take a day trip to Oak Mountain State Park.

Embarking on a day trip to Oak Mountain State Park promises a day filled with outdoor adventure, natural beauty, and recreational activities. As you explore this expansive park, be prepared for a diverse range of landscapes, hiking trails, and opportunities for leisure, making it a perfect destination for nature enthusiasts and outdoor enthusiasts alike.

Start your day trip by planning your activities and choosing specific areas of interest within Oak Mountain State Park. The park is known for its vast size and varied offerings, so having a plan will help you make the most of your visit.

Consider beginning your adventure with a hike along one of the park's scenic trails. Oak Mountain State Park boasts an extensive network of hiking paths, ranging from easy walks to more challenging hikes. Popular trails include the Treetop Nature Trail, the Lake Trail, and the Peavine Falls Trail. Choose a trail that suits your fitness level and desired scenery.

Explore the shores of Double Oak Lake, where you can engage in various water activities. Rent a canoe, kayak, or paddleboard to enjoy a peaceful excursion on the water. Fishing is also a popular activity at the lake, so bring your fishing gear if you're interested in casting a line.

Pack a picnic and enjoy a leisurely lunch at one of the designated picnic areas within the park. Several spots provide picturesque views of the lake or wooded surroundings, creating a serene setting for a meal amidst nature.

Visit the Alabama Wildlife Center, located within the park, to learn about native Alabama wildlife. The center is dedicated to the rehabilitation and conservation of injured and orphaned wild birds. Explore the exhibits and, if timing allows, attend one of the educational programs or presentations.

For those seeking a more adventurous experience, try mountain biking on the park's designated mountain biking trails. The challenging terrain and well-maintained trails make Oak Mountain State Park a popular destination for mountain biking enthusiasts.

If you prefer a relaxing afternoon, explore the scenic driving route within the park. The drive offers panoramic views and allows you to appreciate the natural beauty of the landscape without the need for strenuous physical activity.

Capture the memories of your day trip by taking photographs of the park's landscapes, flora, and fauna. Oak Mountain State Park provides numerous picturesque settings that are worth documenting.

Before concluding your day trip, take a moment to relax and unwind at one of the park's designated rest areas. Reflect on the day's adventures, enjoy the peaceful surroundings, and appreciate the rejuvenating effects of spending time in nature.

Oak Mountain State Park offers a diverse array of activities, ensuring that your day trip can be tailored to your preferences, whether you're seeking adventure, relaxation, or a bit of both. Whether you're a solo adventurer, a nature-loving family, or a group of friends, Oak Mountain State Park provides a memorable and immersive outdoor experience.

# 70. Attend the Birmingham Record Fair.

Attending the Birmingham Record Fair is a music enthusiast's delight, offering a treasure trove of vinyl records, rare finds, and a vibrant atmosphere of musical appreciation. As you immerse yourself in this event, be prepared for a day filled with crate-digging, discovering hidden gems, and connecting with fellow vinyl enthusiasts.

Arrive at the Birmingham Record Fair with a sense of curiosity and an open mind. The fair typically features a diverse range of vendors, each offering their unique collection of vinyl records spanning various genres, eras, and artists.

Explore the booths and tables of the different vendors, carefully flipping through crates of vinyl records. Whether you're on the hunt for rare releases, classic albums, or hidden gems, the fair provides an opportunity to expand your music collection and discover pieces that resonate with your musical tastes.

Engage in conversations with the vendors and fellow record enthusiasts. The Birmingham Record Fair is a community gathering where music lovers come together to share their passion. Exchange recommendations, stories, and insights with others who appreciate the timeless appeal of vinyl records.

Take your time browsing through the records, paying attention to album covers, labels, and any unique editions or pressings. Many vendors bring not only records but also related memorabilia, creating a nostalgic and visually appealing experience for attendees.

Attend any live music performances or DJ sets that may be part of the record fair. Some events feature local musicians or DJs spinning vinyl, adding a live musical element to the atmosphere. Enjoy the soundscape created by the diverse selection of records on display.

Bring a list of specific records you're looking for, but also remain open to serendipitous discoveries. The Birmingham Record Fair is an excellent opportunity to stumble upon albums or artists you may not have considered, expanding your musical horizons.

Check if there are any special promotions, discounts, or exclusive releases offered by vendors. Record fairs often present unique opportunities to snag limited editions or discounted vinyl, making it an exciting experience for collectors.

Consider bringing cash, as some vendors may prefer or only accept cash transactions. Having cash on hand ensures a smooth and convenient shopping experience.

Bring a sturdy bag or crate to carry your vinyl purchases. The fair may present ample opportunities to find new additions to your collection, and having a reliable way to transport your finds is essential.

Before leaving the Birmingham Record Fair, take a moment to appreciate the sense of community and shared love for music. Whether you're a seasoned collector or a newcomer to vinyl culture, the fair provides a space where people come together to celebrate the timeless allure of analog music.

Attending the Birmingham Record Fair is not just about buying records; it's a celebration of music, community, and the tangible, immersive experience of vinyl culture. Whether you're on the hunt for rare vinyl gems or simply want to soak in the atmosphere of like-minded enthusiasts, the record fair promises a day filled with musical exploration and discovery.

# 71.Explore the Birmingham Mural Trail.

Embarking on the Birmingham Mural Trail is a captivating journey through the city's vibrant street art scene. The trail weaves through various neighborhoods, showcasing an array of striking murals that reflect the creativity and cultural expression of local artists. Each mural tells a unique story, contributing to the rich tapestry of Birmingham's urban landscape.

As you follow the trail, be prepared to encounter an eclectic mix of artistic styles, themes, and techniques. From colorful abstract compositions to detailed portraits and thought-provoking social commentary, the murals offer a diverse range of artistic expressions that captivate the observer.

The Birmingham Mural Trail provides a dynamic way to explore different parts of the city, each mural adding its own character to the neighborhood. Take the time to appreciate the details and nuances of each artwork, as they often reflect the history, identity, and aspirations of the community they adorn.

Capture the vibrant scenes with your camera or smartphone, allowing you to share the experience and showcase the talents of the local artists. The murals are not just static paintings; they are dynamic pieces of public art that contribute to the city's evolving cultural identity.

Engage with the local art scene by attending events or festivals related to the Birmingham Mural Trail. Some neighborhoods may host mural unveilings, artist talks, or community gatherings, providing opportunities to connect with fellow art enthusiasts and the creators behind the murals.

Consider the significance of public art in fostering a sense of community and cultural pride. The Birmingham Mural Trail is not just an outdoor art gallery; it's a testament to the city's commitment to creativity, inclusivity, and the transformative power of art in public spaces.

Explore different sections of the trail at various times of the day to experience how natural light and the surrounding environment influence your perception of the murals. Some artworks may reveal hidden details or take on a different mood depending on the time and weather.

Take note of any recurring themes or motifs that emerge as you follow the trail. Whether it's a celebration of local history, a reflection of cultural diversity, or a nod to Birmingham's industrial heritage, these thematic elements contribute to the narrative woven by the murals.

The Birmingham Mural Trail is a living testament to the city's commitment to fostering creativity and enhancing public spaces. It invites residents and visitors alike to engage with art on a large scale, transforming the urban landscape into a dynamic gallery that reflects the spirit and diversity of Birmingham's artistic community.

# 72.Attend the Birmingham Restaurant Week.

Attending Birmingham Restaurant Week is a delightful culinary experience that allows you to savor the diverse and delectable offerings of the city's vibrant dining scene. This annual event typically showcases a variety of local restaurants, each offering special prix-fixe menus or discounts, providing an excellent opportunity to explore new culinary delights and revisit favorite establishments.

Start your culinary adventure by browsing the list of participating restaurants and their respective Birmingham Restaurant Week menus. This curated selection often includes a range of dining options, from casual eateries to upscale establishments, catering to various tastes and preferences.

Consider exploring a mix of cuisines and culinary styles during Birmingham Restaurant Week. Many participating restaurants take this opportunity to showcase their signature dishes or introduce creative, limited-time offerings, allowing you to indulge in a diverse array of flavors.

Make reservations in advance, especially for popular restaurants, to ensure you secure a spot during this busy culinary event. Birmingham Restaurant Week tends to attract locals and visitors alike, creating a lively atmosphere at participating establishments.

Take advantage of the prix-fixe menus or special discounts offered by the restaurants. This allows you to enjoy a multi-course meal or sample a variety of dishes at a more affordable price, making the experience both delicious and cost-effective.

Engage with the local dining community and fellow food enthusiasts during Birmingham Restaurant Week. The event often fosters a sense of camaraderie, with people sharing their culinary discoveries and recommendations. Strike up conversations with restaurant staff and patrons to enhance your dining experience.

Consider exploring neighborhoods or areas of the city that you may not have frequented before. Birmingham Restaurant Week provides an excellent excuse to venture beyond familiar dining spots, discovering hidden gems and culinary treasures in different parts of the city.

Capture the essence of your culinary journey by documenting your dining experiences. Share your favorite dishes, ambiance, and overall impressions on social media, contributing to the celebration of Birmingham's diverse and thriving restaurant scene.

Attend any special events or promotions associated with Birmingham Restaurant Week. Some restaurants may host tastings, chef demonstrations, or other culinary-themed activities during this time, offering additional layers to your overall dining experience.

Express appreciation to the restaurant staff and chefs for their efforts in creating memorable dining experiences. Birmingham Restaurant Week is not only an opportunity for patrons to indulge in exceptional meals but also a chance to acknowledge and support the local hospitality industry.

Whether you're a local resident exploring new flavors or a visitor eager to sample Birmingham's culinary delights, Birmingham Restaurant Week promises a week-long celebration of gastronomy, community, and the city's vibrant food culture.

## 73.Take a hike at Moss Rock Preserve.

Venture onto the trails and immerse yourself in the natural surroundings. Moss Rock Preserve is known for its picturesque moss-covered boulders, which add a distinctive charm to the landscape. Take the time to appreciate the serene ambiance and the soothing sounds of nature as you traverse the well-maintained paths.

Capture the beauty of the preserve through photography. Moss Rock's unique rock formations, wooded areas, and seasonal flora provide ample opportunities to document your hiking experience. Whether you're an avid photographer or simply want to preserve memories, the natural beauty of the preserve is worth capturing.

Consider exploring notable features along the trails, such as the Boulder Field or the Secret Lagoon. These landmarks showcase the geological diversity of Moss Rock Preserve and offer captivating spots to pause, reflect, and appreciate the intricacies of the natural environment.

Respect the preserve's guidelines and practice Leave No Trace principles during your hike. These include staying on designated trails, packing out any waste, and respecting the flora and fauna. By being a responsible hiker, you contribute to the preservation of Moss Rock's ecological integrity.

Bring along essentials for a comfortable hike, including water, appropriate footwear, and sun protection. The trails at Moss Rock Preserve can vary in terrain, so ensuring you have the right gear enhances your overall hiking experience.

Engage in mindfulness as you hike, allowing yourself to be present in the moment and fully absorb the natural beauty surrounding you. Whether you're hiking solo for reflection or with companions for shared experiences, Moss Rock Preserve offers a serene backdrop for connecting with nature.

Take note of the trail markers to ensure you stay on your chosen route. The well-marked trails help guide hikers through the preserve, preventing unintended detours and ensuring a smooth hiking experience.

Before concluding your hike, find a suitable spot to pause, relax, and appreciate the scenic views. Moss Rock Preserve offers several vantage points that allow you to soak in the tranquility of the landscape before heading back to the trailhead.

Exploring Moss Rock Preserve through a hike is not just a physical activity; it's a journey into the natural wonders of Alabama. Whether you're seeking a challenging trail run, a leisurely stroll, or a family-friendly outing, Moss Rock Preserve provides a rejuvenating escape into the great outdoors.

# 74. Attend the Birmingham Fashion Week.

Begin your fashion-filled experience by exploring the event's schedule and lineup of designers. Birmingham Fashion Week often features a diverse range of styles, from avant-garde to ready-to-wear, providing a comprehensive look at the city's fashion landscape.

Secure tickets to the runway shows and events you wish to attend. Birmingham Fashion Week typically includes a series of fashion presentations, designer showcases, and related activities. Purchasing tickets in advance ensures you have a reserved spot to witness the latest trends and designs.

Immerse yourself in the excitement of the runway shows. These curated presentations highlight the talent of local and emerging designers, giving you a front-row seat to the evolving fashion aesthetics within the Birmingham community. Take note of design details, fabric choices, and overall themes presented by the designers.

Engage with the local fashion community by attending networking events or after-parties associated with Birmingham Fashion Week. These gatherings provide opportunities to connect with designers, fashion enthusiasts, and industry professionals, fostering a sense of community within the city's fashion scene.

Capture the essence of the runway and the vibrant atmosphere by documenting your experience through photographs or social media. Birmingham Fashion Week is not only about observing fashion; it's also about sharing your perspective and contributing to the collective celebration of style.

Consider exploring local boutiques and fashion-related businesses during Birmingham Fashion Week. Some events may include pop-up shops or collaborations with retailers, allowing you to discover unique pieces and trends while supporting local businesses.

Dress in your most stylish attire, embracing the opportunity to showcase your personal fashion sense. Birmingham Fashion Week is not just for designers; it's a chance for attendees to express their individual styles and celebrate the diversity of fashion within the community.

Attend any panel discussions or fashion-related talks that may be part of Birmingham Fashion Week's programming. These sessions often feature insights from industry professionals, designers, or influencers, providing a deeper understanding of the fashion landscape in Birmingham and beyond.

Express appreciation for the designers and organizers involved in Birmingham Fashion Week. Whether through social media, direct feedback, or supporting local designers, acknowledging the creative contributions enhances the sense of community within the city's fashion ecosystem.

Participating in Birmingham Fashion Week is not just about observing trends; it's a collective celebration of creativity, self-expression, and the evolving fashion culture within the city. Whether you're a seasoned fashion enthusiast or a newcomer to the scene, Birmingham Fashion Week offers an exciting opportunity to witness the intersection of art and style in the Magic City.

# 75.Explore the Liberty Park Sports Complex.

Engage in a game of tennis or pickleball at the dedicated courts within the complex. Whether you're a seasoned player or a beginner, the well-maintained courts offer a welcoming environment to enjoy these racquet sports. Consider bringing your own equipment or checking if rentals are available on-site.

Explore the walking trails and green spaces surrounding the sports complex. Liberty Park often features scenic trails that provide a refreshing outdoor experience. Whether you prefer a brisk walk, jog, or a leisurely stroll, the trails offer a chance to connect with nature and stay active.

Discover the diverse sports fields available for activities like soccer, baseball, softball, and more. The Liberty Park Sports Complex is designed to accommodate various team sports, making it a hub for local leagues, tournaments, and recreational games. If interested, check the schedule to see if any events or games are taking place during your visit.

Take advantage of the open spaces for activities like frisbee, picnics, or simply enjoying the outdoors. Many visitors find the Liberty Park Sports Complex to be an ideal spot for family outings, group gatherings, or solo relaxation in a green and well-maintained setting.

Bring along sports equipment such as soccer balls, footballs, or frisbees for impromptu games on the open fields. Liberty Park encourages a sense of community and active living, making it an excellent location for both organized sports and casual recreational activities.

Check if there are any community events or sports clinics happening at the complex. Liberty Park may host sports-related programs, youth camps, or fitness classes, providing additional opportunities to engage with the local sports community.

Consider packing a picnic and enjoying a meal in the designated areas within the complex. Some parks offer picnic tables, benches, or grassy areas where you can relax and refuel after a day of sports and outdoor activities.

Capture the moments of your exploration through photographs. The Liberty Park Sports Complex offers scenic backdrops, whether it's the vibrant sports fields, the surrounding nature, or the camaraderie of fellow sports enthusiasts. Documenting your visit allows you to share the experience with others and create lasting memories.

Before leaving, take a moment to appreciate the sense of community and active living fostered by the Liberty Park Sports Complex. Whether you're participating in organized sports, enjoying a leisurely walk, or simply soaking in the outdoor atmosphere, the complex serves as a hub for recreation and a gathering place for those who appreciate an active and healthy lifestyle.

# 76.Attend the Funky Fish Fry at the Birmingham Zoo.

Begin your Funky Fish Fry experience by checking the event details and schedule. The zoo typically hosts this lively affair with a focus on seafood offerings, live music, and family-friendly activities. Ensure you have your tickets and any additional information about the event.

Explore the diverse array of seafood options at the Funky Fish Fry. From classic fish and chips to creative seafood dishes, the event often features a variety of culinary delights prepared by local chefs. Embrace the opportunity to savor the flavors of the sea in a fun and festive setting.

Enjoy the lively atmosphere created by live music or entertainment that accompanies the Funky Fish Fry. Whether it's a local band, DJ, or other performers, the event aims to provide a soundtrack that complements the celebratory vibe. Dance, sing along, or simply groove to the tunes as you indulge in the seafood delights.

Take a leisurely stroll through the zoo during the Funky Fish Fry. Some areas of the zoo may be open for exploration during the event, allowing you to enjoy the exhibits and observe the animals in the unique ambiance of an evening gathering.

Consider attending with family or friends, as the Funky Fish Fry is designed to be a social and communal experience. The combination of good food, music, and the zoo's charming atmosphere creates a festive setting for shared enjoyment.

Capture the moments of your Funky Fish Fry experience through photographs. The colorful displays, vibrant atmosphere, and perhaps even some of the zoo's residents contribute to a visually appealing backdrop. Documenting your time at the event allows you to share the fun with others and create lasting memories.

Participate in any interactive or family-friendly activities that may be part of the Funky Fish Fry. The event organizers often include games, face painting, or other amusements suitable for attendees of all ages, making it a well-rounded experience for families and individuals alike.

Embrace the opportunity to support local businesses and vendors that may be part of the Funky Fish Fry. From seafood providers to artisans or merchandise stalls, the event often showcases a variety of offerings from the community.

Before concluding your evening, take a moment to soak in the ambiance of the Funky Fish Fry. Whether you're savoring the last bites of seafood, enjoying the music, or simply appreciating the unique setting, the event provides a festive and laid-back experience within the lively backdrop of the Birmingham Zoo.

Attending the Funky Fish Fry at the Birmingham Zoo is not just a culinary adventure; it's a celebration of community, entertainment, and the joy of gathering in a unique and lively setting. Whether you're a seafood enthusiast, a music lover, or someone seeking a family-friendly outing, the Funky Fish Fry offers a blend of flavors and fun against the backdrop of the zoo's charming ambiance.

# 77.Take a stroll through the Birmingham Farmers Market.

Begin your journey by arriving at the Birmingham Farmers Market during its operational hours. Markets often take place on designated days, offering a prime opportunity to discover locally sourced products and engage with local vendors.

Wander through the market stalls and appreciate the colorful displays of fresh fruits, vegetables, and seasonal produce. Local farmers and growers often showcase their best offerings, providing a chance to connect with the agricultural community and purchase high-quality, locally sourced ingredients.

Engage with local artisans and vendors offering a variety of handmade goods. From artisanal bread and cheeses to handcrafted jewelry and artwork, the Birmingham Farmers Market is a treasure trove of unique and locally produced items. Take the time to explore these offerings and support the creativity of local entrepreneurs.

Immerse yourself in the lively atmosphere of the market. Many farmers markets feature live music, food vendors, and community activities. Enjoy the sounds of local musicians, indulge in delicious treats from food stands, and appreciate the sense of community that permeates the market setting.

Sample local and regional specialties. Farmers markets often feature vendors offering ready-to-eat items or food samples. Take advantage of the opportunity to try new flavors and culinary creations, contributing to the overall sensory experience of the market.

Bring a reusable bag or basket to carry your purchases. The Birmingham Farmers Market is an eco-friendly environment, and bringing your own bag helps reduce waste and makes it easier to transport your fresh finds.

Take note of the seasonal offerings and events happening at the market. Depending on the time of year, the market may host special events, themed markets, or seasonal celebrations. Participating in these activities adds an extra layer of enjoyment to your market experience.

Engage in conversations with local farmers and vendors. Learning about the products, cultivation methods, and stories behind the offerings enhances your connection to the community and provides insights into the local agricultural landscape.

Capture the vibrant scenes and unique moments through photography. Whether it's the colorful produce displays, the friendly interactions between vendors and customers, or the overall market ambiance, documenting your stroll through the Birmingham Farmers Market allows you to share the experience and celebrate the local community.

Before concluding your visit, take a moment to appreciate the sense of community and connection fostered by the Birmingham Farmers Market. Supporting local farmers, artisans, and businesses contributes to the sustainability of the local economy and allows you to be part of the vibrant tapestry of the Birmingham community.

# 78.Attend a performance by the Alabama Symphony Orchestra.

Start your experience by checking the schedule and program details for the Alabama Symphony Orchestra's upcoming performance. Familiarize yourself with the pieces that will be featured, the venue, and any additional information that enhances your understanding of the musical journey you're about to embark on.

Dress appropriately for the occasion, embracing the opportunity to enjoy a night of classical elegance. Attending an orchestra performance often calls for semi-formal or formal attire, contributing to the overall ambiance of the evening.

Arrive early to the venue to allow time for parking, ticket retrieval, and finding your seat. Many orchestra performances begin with pre-concert talks or other activities that provide insights into the featured compositions. Taking advantage of these offerings enhances your appreciation for the music.

Engage with the program notes provided or available online. Understanding the context, history, and nuances of the musical pieces adds depth to your experience. Whether you're a seasoned classical music enthusiast or a first-time attendee, gaining insights into the compositions enriches your connection to the performance.

Silence your mobile devices before the performance begins to ensure an undisturbed and immersive experience. The Alabama Symphony Orchestra performances often create an atmosphere of collective focus, allowing the audience to fully engage with the beauty and complexity of the music.

Immerse yourself in the symphonic journey as the musicians bring the compositions to life. Pay attention to the conductor's cues, the interplay of different sections of the orchestra, and the dynamic range of emotions conveyed through the music. Allow yourself to be transported by the expressive power of the orchestra.

Consider attending post-concert events if available, such as meet-and-greet sessions with the musicians or discussions about the performance. These opportunities provide a chance to connect with the performers, gain further insights into the music, and share your enthusiasm for the experience.

Applaud and show appreciation for the musicians at the conclusion of each piece and the overall performance. The interaction between the audience and the orchestra creates a shared appreciation for the artistry and dedication of the performers.

Reflect on your experience after the performance. Consider how the music made you feel, the emotions it evoked, and the lasting impressions it left. Whether you're moved by the grandeur of a symphony or the subtleties of a chamber piece, attending an Alabama Symphony Orchestra performance is a journey of musical discovery and emotional resonance.

Attending a performance by the Alabama Symphony Orchestra is not just a night out; it's an opportunity to witness the collective talent and passion of exceptional musicians. Whether you're a seasoned classical music aficionado or a newcomer to orchestral performances, the Alabama Symphony Orchestra promises an enriching and memorable cultural experience.

# 79.Explore the 20th Street North Historic District.

Begin your journey by strolling along 20th Street North and taking in the architectural beauty of the historic buildings that line the district. Many of these structures date back to the early 20th century, showcasing a range of architectural styles, including Beaux-Arts and Classical Revival. Admire the details of facades, ornate cornices, and historic signage that contribute to the district's character.

Visit the Alabama Theatre, a notable landmark in the 20th Street North Historic District. This historic theater, dating back to 1927, is renowned for its grand architecture and serves as a cultural hub for film screenings, concerts, and events. Check the schedule to see if any performances or screenings align with your visit.

Explore the diverse array of businesses that call the district home. From boutique shops and art galleries to restaurants and cafes, the 20th Street North Historic District offers a mix of retail and culinary experiences. Take the time to browse through local stores and support the unique offerings of the district's businesses.

Capture the vibrant street scenes and architectural details through photography. The juxtaposition of historic buildings with modern elements and the bustling urban environment creates visually appealing compositions. Documenting your exploration allows you to share the charm of the 20th Street North Historic District with others.

Visit Linn Park, which is adjacent to the district. This centrally located park provides a green oasis in the heart of downtown Birmingham. Take a leisurely stroll, relax on a bench, or appreciate the park's historical monuments and statues, including the Confederate Soldiers and Sailors Monument.

Consider exploring the district during special events or festivals. Depending on the time of your visit, the 20th Street North Historic District may host community events, art walks, or cultural celebrations. Participating in these activities provides an opportunity to engage with the local community and experience the district in a dynamic setting.

Learn about the history of the district through interpretive plaques or guided tours, if available. Gain insights into the evolution of Birmingham and the role of the 20th Street North area in the city's development. Understanding the historical context enhances your appreciation for the district's significance.

Dine at one of the district's restaurants to experience Birmingham's culinary scene. Many establishments in the 20th Street North Historic District offer diverse menus, ranging from Southern comfort food to international cuisine. Enjoy a meal in a historic setting or opt for outdoor seating to soak in the urban ambiance.

Reflect on the dynamic synergy between the historic and contemporary elements of the 20th Street North Historic District. Whether you're drawn to the architectural splendor, the local businesses, or the cultural happenings, this district encapsulates the spirit of Birmingham's past and present.

# 80.Attend the Birmingham Hammerfest.

Begin your Hammerfest experience by checking the event schedule and race routes. The Birmingham Hammerfest typically features various races, including criteriums and road races, with cyclists navigating through the city streets and surrounding areas. Familiarizing yourself with the details ensures you can plan your attendance and catch the races that interest you.

Position yourself strategically along the race route to witness the cyclists speeding by. Whether you choose a spot near the starting line, a challenging uphill section, or the thrilling final sprint, each location offers a unique perspective on the intensity and strategy of competitive cycling.

Bring a chair or blanket for comfortable viewing, especially if you plan to spend an extended period enjoying the races. Many spectators choose popular vantage points to witness multiple laps or stages of the competition, creating a festive and communal atmosphere.

Embrace the energetic ambiance of the Birmingham Hammerfest as spectators cheer on the cyclists. The race's dynamic nature, with fast-paced sprints and strategic maneuvers, adds to the excitement. Engage with fellow spectators, cyclists, and event organizers to immerse yourself in the cycling community.

Consider exploring the event's surrounding festivities, if available. The Birmingham Hammerfest may include vendor booths, cycling-related activities, or food and beverage options. These add-ons contribute to the overall enjoyment of the event and provide a well-rounded experience for attendees.

Capture the thrilling moments of the races through photography or videos. The speed, agility, and determination of the cyclists make for compelling visuals. Documenting the Birmingham Hammerfest allows you to relive the excitement and share your perspective with others.

If possible, attend any awards ceremonies or podium celebrations to congratulate the winning cyclists and appreciate their achievements. These moments often provide insights into the competitive spirit and camaraderie within the cycling community.

Support local businesses in the vicinity of the race route. Many shops and cafes may offer special promotions or cycling-themed events during the Birmingham Hammerfest. Exploring the local scene adds to the vibrancy of your overall experience.

Check for any community events or cycling-related activities scheduled alongside the Birmingham Hammerfest. The event may coincide with bike rides, expos, or workshops, providing additional opportunities to engage with the cycling culture and community.

Reflect on the athleticism, strategy, and sheer determination displayed by the cyclists during the Birmingham Hammerfest. Whether you're a seasoned cycling enthusiast or a newcomer to the sport, attending this event offers a thrilling glimpse into the world of competitive cycling and underscores the sense of community fostered by the Birmingham cycling scene.

# 81.Take a pottery class at Red Dot Gallery.

Start your pottery class by checking the schedule and availability at Red Dot Gallery. Classes may vary in duration and focus, so choose a session that aligns with your interests and schedule. It's advisable to register in advance to secure your spot in the class.

Arrive at the gallery with an open mind and a willingness to learn. Red Dot Gallery's pottery classes are often designed for participants of all skill levels, from beginners to more experienced potters. The instructors at the gallery are typically experienced artists who guide participants through the process of creating pottery.

Wear appropriate clothing for a pottery class, as working with clay can be a hands-on and sometimes messy experience. Aprons or old clothes are recommended to protect against splatters and clay residue.

Familiarize yourself with the studio space and the tools provided for the class. Red Dot Gallery is likely to have well-equipped pottery studios with pottery wheels, clay, sculpting tools, and glazes. Take a moment to acquaint yourself with the materials you'll be working with during the class.

Listen attentively to the instructor's guidance and demonstrations. Red Dot Gallery's instructors are there to support and guide you through the pottery-making process. Pay attention to techniques, tips, and safety guidelines to make the most of your creative experience.

Engage with fellow participants during the class. Pottery classes often create a collaborative and supportive atmosphere. Share ideas, ask questions, and enjoy the camaraderie of creating alongside other art enthusiasts.

Experiment with different techniques and shapes as you work on your pottery project. Whether you're throwing clay on a wheel or hand-building a unique piece, embrace the opportunity to explore your creativity under the guidance of the instructor.

Take breaks when needed and step back to assess your work. Pottery is a process that requires patience and attention to detail. Allow yourself to enjoy the journey of creating something with your hands.

Experience the satisfaction of completing your pottery project. Red Dot Gallery's classes typically culminate in the firing and glazing of the finished pieces. Witnessing the transformation of raw clay into a finished ceramic piece is a rewarding and fulfilling aspect of the pottery-making process.

Consider attending any gallery exhibitions or events at Red Dot Gallery to further immerse yourself in the local art scene. Red Dot Gallery often showcases works by local artists, providing additional inspiration and a chance to appreciate the broader artistic community.

Reflect on your pottery class experience and the creative journey you undertook at Red Dot Gallery. Whether you're a novice or a seasoned artist, the class offers a unique opportunity to connect with the artistic process and express yourself through the medium of clay.

# 82.Explore the Birmingham Originals Restaurant Week.

Start your exploration by checking the schedule and participating restaurants for Birmingham Originals Restaurant Week. The event typically features a curated list of independent, locally-owned restaurants offering special prix-fixe menus or discounts. Familiarize yourself with the offerings and plan your dining experiences accordingly.

Choose a variety of restaurants to visit during the week. Birmingham Originals Restaurant Week often includes a diverse selection of eateries, ranging from fine dining establishments to casual gems. Consider exploring different cuisines and culinary styles to fully experience the richness of Birmingham's local food scene.

# Travel to Birmingham Alabama

Make reservations in advance, especially for popular restaurants. Birmingham Originals Restaurant Week attracts food enthusiasts, and securing a reservation ensures you have a spot at your chosen dining destination. Many participating restaurants offer special menus or discounts exclusively for this event.

Explore the special menus created for Birmingham Originals Restaurant Week. These menus often showcase the restaurant's signature dishes or feature unique creations specifically crafted for the event. Take advantage of the opportunity to try new flavors and culinary delights.

Engage with the restaurant staff and chefs to learn more about the locally sourced ingredients and the inspiration behind the dishes. Birmingham Originals Restaurant Week is an excellent time to connect with the people who make the local culinary scene thrive and gain insights into the creative processes behind each dish.

Attend any special events or promotions associated with Birmingham Originals Restaurant Week. Some restaurants may host tastings, chef's dinners, or other activities to enhance the dining experience. Participating in these events provides an extra layer of enjoyment and allows you to engage more deeply with the local food culture.

Consider exploring different neighborhoods in Birmingham during Restaurant Week. Each area of the city has its own unique character, and Birmingham Originals Restaurant Week provides an opportunity to discover hidden culinary gems in various parts of town.

Document your culinary journey through photographs and share your experiences on social media. Many restaurants participating in Birmingham Originals Restaurant Week take pride in their presentation, and sharing your dining adventures contributes to the promotion of local businesses and the event itself.

Reflect on the week-long dining experience and the array of flavors you encountered. Birmingham Originals Restaurant Week not only allows you to indulge in delicious meals but also supports the local economy and celebrates the independent spirit of Birmingham's culinary scene. Whether you're a local resident or a visitor, this event offers a delectable exploration of the city's diverse and thriving restaurant landscape.

# 83.Attend a Birmingham Children's Theatre production.

Start by checking the schedule of upcoming productions at the Birmingham Children's Theatre. The theater often features a diverse lineup of shows, ranging from classic fairy tales to contemporary stories. Choose a production that aligns with the interests and age group of the children attending, and consider purchasing tickets in advance to secure your seats.

Arrive at the theater early to allow time for parking, ticket pickup, and finding your seats. The Birmingham Children's Theatre typically provides a welcoming and family-friendly atmosphere, with staff ready to assist you in making the most of your theater experience.

Engage with the pre-show activities and interactive elements, if available. Some productions may include pre-show events, character meet-and-greets, or hands-on activities designed to enhance the overall experience for young theatergoers. Take advantage of these opportunities to create a more immersive and enjoyable outing.

Encourage children to participate in the excitement of live theater. The Birmingham Children's Theatre often welcomes audience interaction, allowing children to respond to the performance with laughter, applause, and even the occasional shout of excitement. Embrace the lively and inclusive atmosphere of the theater.

Capture the moments through photographs or videos, respecting any guidelines provided by the theater. Documenting the experience allows you to preserve the memories of the theatrical outing and share the excitement with friends and family.

Discuss the production with the children after the show. Explore their thoughts, feelings, and favorite moments. Encourage them to express their impressions of the characters, storyline, and the magic of live theater. This post-show reflection enhances the overall educational and entertainment value of the experience.

Consider exploring any post-show activities or workshops offered by the Birmingham Children's Theatre. Some productions may include opportunities for children to engage further with the themes of the show or participate in theater-related activities. Check for any additional programming to extend the theatrical experience.

Support the Birmingham Children's Theatre by considering memberships, donations, or future attendance. The theater plays a vital role in the cultural and educational development of young audiences, and your ongoing support helps ensure the continuation of quality productions and programming.

Reflect on the joy and wonder experienced during the Birmingham Children's Theatre production. Whether it's the enchanting storytelling, colorful characters, or the magic of live performance, attending a production at the Birmingham Children's Theatre creates lasting memories and cultivates a love for the arts in the hearts of young audience members.

# 84. Take a scenic drive along Cahaba Beach Road.

Begin your drive by accessing Cahaba Beach Road and taking a moment to appreciate the change in scenery from urban to natural surroundings. The road is known for its scenic qualities, so leisurely driving allows you to absorb the beauty of the area.

Roll down your windows to embrace the fresh air and listen to the sounds of nature as you drive. The gentle rustle of leaves, bird songs, and the murmur of nearby water contribute to the soothing ambiance along Cahaba Beach Road.

Observe the Cahaba River, which the road parallels. The river is known for its biodiversity and is home to various plant and animal species. Take breaks at designated overlooks or safe spots to enjoy the river views and perhaps capture some photographs.

Keep an eye out for wildlife. Cahaba Beach Road and the surrounding area are habitats for diverse fauna. Depending on the time of day and season, you may spot birds, turtles, and other wildlife along the route. Drive with caution, especially in areas where animals may cross the road.

Explore any designated recreational areas or parks along Cahaba Beach Road. These areas may offer opportunities for hiking, picnicking, or simply enjoying the outdoors. Check for trailheads or access points that allow you to stretch your legs and immerse yourself further in the natural surroundings.

Consider timing your drive to coincide with sunrise or sunset for a magical play of light and shadows across the landscape. The changing colors of the sky, combined with the scenic backdrop, enhance the visual appeal of the drive and create a serene and memorable experience.

Respect the natural environment and follow any guidelines or regulations in place to preserve the beauty of Cahaba Beach Road. Stay on designated paths, dispose of litter responsibly, and appreciate the delicate balance of the ecosystem.

Connect with fellow nature enthusiasts by researching local nature groups or events that may involve Cahaba Beach Road. Participating in guided nature walks or activities adds a social dimension to your exploration and allows you to learn more about the area from knowledgeable guides.

Reflect on the tranquility and natural splendor experienced during your scenic drive along Cahaba Beach Road. Whether you're seeking a peaceful retreat, a connection with nature, or a scenic drive, this route offers a refreshing escape from the urban landscape and a chance to appreciate the beauty of Alabama's natural surroundings.

# 85.Attend the Birmingham Arts and Music Festival.

Start by checking the festival schedule and lineup to plan your visit. The Birmingham Arts and Music Festival often features a variety of events, including live music performances, art exhibitions, workshops, and interactive activities. Familiarize yourself with the schedule to ensure you don't miss out on any highlights.

Explore the different venues and stages hosting performances and exhibits. The festival may take place in various locations throughout Birmingham, providing an opportunity to discover new artistic spaces and venues. Consider creating a personalized itinerary to make the most of your time at the festival.

Engage with the local arts community by attending art exhibitions and installations. The Birmingham Arts and Music Festival typically highlights the work of local visual artists, offering a chance to explore a wide range of artistic styles and mediums. Take the time to appreciate the creativity on display and consider supporting local artists by purchasing their work.

Immerse yourself in the live music performances scheduled throughout the festival. Birmingham has a rich musical heritage, and the festival often features a diverse lineup of genres and artists. Whether you're a fan of jazz, rock, blues, or indie music, the festival provides an opportunity to discover and enjoy the sounds of the local music scene.

Participate in any interactive workshops or demonstrations offered during the festival. Some events may provide hands-on experiences, allowing you to connect with artists, musicians, and fellow festival-goers. Whether it's a painting workshop, a music jam session, or a dance class, these activities enhance your engagement with the creative community.

Capture the vibrant moments of the festival through photography or videos. Documenting your experience allows you to relive the excitement and share the highlights with friends and family. Be respectful of performers and fellow attendees when taking photos.

Interact with the local community and fellow festival-goers. The Birmingham Arts and Music Festival fosters a sense of camaraderie and community spirit. Strike up conversations, share your enthusiasm for the arts, and connect with like-minded individuals who appreciate the cultural richness of Birmingham.

Support local businesses and vendors at the festival. Explore food stalls, artisan markets, and local businesses participating in the event. Purchasing goods and services from local vendors contributes to the economic vitality of the community.

Reflect on the diversity of artistic expressions and the cultural vibrancy experienced during the Birmingham Arts and Music Festival. Whether you're a seasoned arts enthusiast or a newcomer to the scene, this festival offers a dynamic and immersive celebration of creativity, showcasing the talent and passion that define Birmingham's arts and music community.

# 86.Explore the Historic Fountain Heights neighborhood.

Begin your exploration by strolling through the residential streets of Historic Fountain Heights. Take note of the architectural diversity, ranging from historic homes with unique character to more contemporary structures. The neighborhood is known for its mix of architectural styles, showcasing the evolution of Birmingham over the years.

Visit the historic landmarks that contribute to the neighborhood's cultural heritage. Fountain Heights is home to several churches, schools, and community buildings with historical significance. Pay attention to architectural details and plaques that provide insights into the stories and events associated with these landmarks.

Explore Kelly Ingram Park, located near the southern edge of Fountain Heights. This park is an important historical site and played a significant role in the Civil Rights Movement. Admire the sculptures and monuments that commemorate the struggle for civil rights and take a moment to reflect on the park's historical importance.

Engage with the local community by visiting neighborhood businesses and shops. Historic Fountain Heights is likely to have locally-owned establishments that contribute to the area's unique character. Consider supporting these businesses, whether it's grabbing a cup of coffee or browsing through local boutiques.

Attend community events or activities that may be taking place in Historic Fountain Heights. Neighborhood gatherings, cultural festivals, or historic tours offer opportunities to connect with residents, learn more about the area, and immerse yourself in the community spirit.

Capture the charm of the neighborhood through photography. Document the architectural details, tree-lined streets, and any public art or murals that contribute to the visual appeal of Historic Fountain Heights. Share your images to showcase the neighborhood's beauty with others.

Learn about the history of Fountain Heights by researching its origins and development. Understand how the neighborhood has evolved over time, from its early days to its role in the Civil Rights Movement. Local historical societies or community centers may provide resources or guided tours to enhance your knowledge.

Reflect on the sense of community and history experienced during your exploration of Historic Fountain Heights. Consider the stories embedded in the architecture, the resilience of the community, and the cultural richness that defines this neighborhood. Whether you're a history enthusiast or someone seeking to connect with a vibrant community, Historic Fountain Heights offers a meaningful and engaging experience.

# 87. Attend the Do It Downtown Festival.

Start your day by checking the schedule and lineup of events for the Do It Downtown Festival. The festival may include live music performances, art installations, food vendors, and various interactive activities. Familiarize yourself with the program to plan your itinerary and ensure you don't miss out on any highlights.

Explore the different areas and attractions within downtown Birmingham that are part of the festival. The event may span multiple blocks or venues, allowing you to discover new spaces and experience the unique character of downtown. Consider creating a flexible plan to make the most of your time and cover various festival offerings.

Engage with local artists and performers showcasing their talents during the festival. From street performers to live art demonstrations, the Do It Downtown Festival provides a platform for the city's creative community. Take the time to appreciate the diverse expressions of art and culture on display.

Participate in interactive activities or workshops offered as part of the festival. These may include art and craft stations, DIY projects, or community engagement initiatives. Embrace the opportunity to connect with fellow festival-goers and contribute to the collective spirit of the event.

Indulge in the culinary offerings from food vendors or nearby restaurants participating in the festival. Downtown Birmingham is likely to have a diverse array of culinary delights, and the festival provides a chance to savor local flavors. Consider trying something new or enjoying a favorite dish from a local eatery.

Enjoy live music performances at designated stages or venues. The Do It Downtown Festival often features a lineup of local bands or musicians, contributing to the lively atmosphere of the event. Whether you're a fan of a specific genre or open to discovering new sounds, the musical offerings add to the festival's appeal.

Connect with the local community and fellow festival-goers. The Do It Downtown Festival fosters a sense of camaraderie and community spirit. Strike up conversations, share your enthusiasm for the festivities, and immerse yourself in the shared experience of celebrating downtown Birmingham.

Capture the vibrant moments of the festival through photography or videos. Documenting your experience allows you to relive the excitement and share the highlights with friends and family. Be sure to respect performers and fellow attendees when taking photos.

Reflect on the energy, creativity, and community spirit experienced during the Do It Downtown Festival. Whether you're a local resident or a visitor, this festival offers a lively and immersive celebration of downtown Birmingham, showcasing the city's cultural richness and the dynamic spirit that defines its downtown scene.

# 88. Take a horseback riding tour at Griffin Farms.

Start your horseback riding tour by checking in at Griffin Farms and familiarizing yourself with the staff and facilities. The farm is likely to provide trained guides and well-cared-for horses to ensure a safe and enjoyable experience.

Receive a brief orientation and safety instructions from the guides. Pay attention to guidelines on mounting, dismounting, and controlling your horse. Griffin Farms prioritizes the safety of riders and horses, so adherence to these instructions enhances the overall experience.

Meet your horse and take a moment to establish a connection. Some farms encourage a brief introduction between riders and their horses to build trust and familiarity. This interaction contributes to a more enjoyable and comfortable ride.

Embark on the horseback riding tour, following designated trails that showcase the natural beauty of Griffin Farms. Enjoy the scenery, which may include open fields, wooded areas, and possibly even water features. The farm setting adds an extra layer of charm to the riding experience.

Listen to the guidance of your horseback riding guide. They are likely to share interesting information about the farm, its history, and the surrounding environment. Feel free to ask questions and engage with the guide to enhance your understanding of the area.

Capture the scenic moments of your horseback riding tour through photography, respecting any guidelines provided by the farm. Documenting your experience allows you to relive the beauty of the ride and share the memories with others.

Take breaks during the tour to appreciate the surroundings and give your horse a moment to rest. Griffin Farms may have designated spots for rest or points of interest along the trail. Use these breaks to soak in the peaceful atmosphere and enjoy the farm's natural elements.

Follow any additional activities or experiences offered by Griffin Farms. Some farms may provide options for longer rides, group tours, or even themed rides. Explore these possibilities to customize your horseback riding adventure based on your preferences.

Express gratitude to the guides and staff at Griffin Farms for providing a memorable experience. Consider leaving feedback or reviews to contribute to the farm's reputation and help future visitors make informed decisions.

Reflect on the tranquility and beauty experienced during your horseback riding tour at Griffin Farms. Whether you're a novice rider or an experienced equestrian, this outdoor excursion offers a peaceful connection with nature and the joy of exploring the scenic trails on horseback.

## 89.Attend the Birmingham Air Show.

Start your day by checking the schedule and lineup of performances for the Birmingham Air Show. The event may include a variety of aircraft, from military jets to aerobatic planes, showcasing the skill and precision of pilots. Familiarize yourself with the program to plan your day and ensure you don't miss any of the high-flying action.

Arrive at the air show venue early to secure a good viewing spot. Many air shows offer designated areas for spectators to set up chairs or blankets, providing a comfortable vantage point for enjoying the aerial displays. Consider bringing sunscreen, hats, and other necessities for a day spent outdoors.

Engage with static displays and exhibits showcasing different aircraft on the ground. The Birmingham Air Show often includes opportunities for attendees to get up close to various airplanes, helicopters, and military vehicles. Take the time to explore these exhibits and learn more about the featured aircraft.

Prepare to be amazed by the aerobatic performances and precision flying demonstrations. Aerobatic teams may execute breathtaking maneuvers, including loops, rolls, and daring formations. Capture the moments through photography or simply enjoy the spectacle as skilled pilots push the limits of flight.

Listen to the commentary and narration during the air show, providing insights into the aircraft, pilots, and the history of aviation. Gain a deeper appreciation for the technical skill and expertise required for each aerial performance. Some air shows also feature interviews with pilots, adding a personal touch to the event.

Bring binoculars for a closer view of the aircraft in action. While many air shows are designed to provide a thrilling experience for spectators on the ground, binoculars can enhance your ability to appreciate the details of aerobatic maneuvers and formations.

Stay hydrated and pack snacks to keep yourself energized throughout the day. Air shows can be physically demanding, and having water and snacks on hand ensures you stay comfortable and focused on enjoying the performances.

Capture memories of the air show by taking photographs or videos. Documenting the impressive aerial displays allows you to relive the excitement and share your experience with others. Be sure to adhere to any rules or guidelines regarding photography set by the air show organizers.

Connect with fellow aviation enthusiasts and spectators. Air shows often attract a diverse crowd of individuals passionate about aviation. Strike up conversations, share your excitement, and enjoy the communal atmosphere of the event.

Reflect on the day's experiences and the breathtaking displays witnessed during the Birmingham Air Show. Whether you're a seasoned aviation enthusiast or attending your first air show, this event offers a thrilling and memorable celebration of flight, precision, and the marvels of the sky.

# 90. Explore the historic Glen Iris Park neighborhood.

Begin your exploration in Glen Iris Park by wandering through its tree-shaded streets adorned with well-preserved historic homes. Many of these residences showcase various architectural styles popular in the early to mid-20th century, providing a visual feast for architecture enthusiasts and history buffs alike.

Take a stroll through the central park or green spaces within the neighborhood. These areas often serve as gathering spots for residents and add to the overall tranquility of Glen Iris Park. You might encounter locals walking their dogs, enjoying a picnic, or simply appreciating the peaceful ambiance.

Visit the historic Glen Iris Park itself, if one exists. Parks are often focal points in neighborhoods, offering green spaces for recreation and relaxation. Learn about the history of the park, any landmarks within it, and enjoy the natural surroundings.

Engage with the local community by checking out nearby shops, cafes, or community centers. Glen Iris Park may have local businesses that contribute to the neighborhood's character. Consider striking up conversations with residents or business owners to gain insights into the area's unique charm.

Explore any community events or gatherings that might be taking place. Neighborhoods like Glen Iris Park often host events, farmers' markets, or festivals that bring residents together. Participating in these activities provides an opportunity to connect with the community and experience local culture.

Capture the beauty of the neighborhood through photography. Document the architecture, landscapes, and any notable landmarks you encounter during your exploration. This allows you to create lasting memories of your visit and share the charm of Glen Iris Park with others.

If there are historical markers or plaques, take a moment to read about the history of Glen Iris Park. Many neighborhoods have interesting stories about their development, notable residents, or significant events that shaped their identity.

Consider exploring nearby attractions, as Glen Iris Park is often situated close to points of interest. In Birmingham, you might find yourself near cultural institutions, museums, or parks that add to the overall appeal of the area.

Reflect on the sense of history and community spirit experienced during your exploration of the Glen Iris Park neighborhood. Whether you're admiring the architecture, enjoying the green spaces, or interacting with locals, historic neighborhoods like Glen Iris Park often offer a blend of character and community that makes them special.

# 91.Attend the Birmingham Carnival.

Start your day at the Birmingham Carnival by checking the event schedule and lineup. Carnivals often feature a variety of activities, including parades, live music, dance performances, vibrant costumes, and delicious food. Familiarize yourself with the program to plan your day and ensure you don't miss any of the exciting festivities.

Witness the colorful and energetic parade, a highlight of many carnivals. Admire the elaborate costumes, lively music, and enthusiastic dancers as they make their way through the streets of Birmingham. The parade is likely to showcase the diversity and creativity of the local community.

Explore the carnival grounds, where you'll find an array of food stalls offering delicious treats from various cultures. Indulge in carnival favorites, exotic dishes, and international cuisines that contribute to the gastronomic delights of the event.

Immerse yourself in the cultural performances and entertainment scheduled throughout the day. From traditional dances to live music, the Birmingham Carnival is sure to feature a diverse lineup that celebrates the rich heritage of the community. Find a comfortable spot to enjoy the performances and embrace the rhythmic beats.

Engage with interactive activities and games that capture the spirit of the carnival. From face painting and mask-making to carnival rides and games, there's likely to be something for attendees of all ages. Participate in the festivities and create lasting memories.

Capture the vibrant moments of the Birmingham Carnival through photography or videos. Documenting the colorful costumes, dynamic performances, and joyful expressions allows you to relive the excitement and share the carnival experience with others.

Connect with fellow carnival-goers and embrace the sense of community spirit. Carnivals often bring people together, providing an opportunity to celebrate diversity, share cultural experiences, and enjoy a day of fun and camaraderie.

Respect the cultural significance of the Birmingham Carnival by learning about its traditions and the communities it represents. Carnivals often carry historical and cultural meanings, and taking the time to understand and appreciate these aspects enhances the overall experience.

Reflect on the joy, vibrancy, and cultural richness experienced during your time at the Birmingham Carnival. Whether you're dancing to the beats, savoring international flavors, or simply soaking in the festive atmosphere, the carnival offers a unique and memorable celebration of community and culture.

# 92. Take a historic tour of the Boyles House.

Begin your historic tour of the Boyles House by stepping through its distinguished entrance. This historic home, known for its architectural charm, likely boasts features that reflect the era in which it was built. From the facade to the intricate details, observe the craftsmanship that has withstood the test of time.

Meet your knowledgeable tour guide, who may share the history of the Boyles House and its connection to Birmingham's past. Learn about the original owners, the architectural style, and any notable events or individuals associated with the residence. The guide may provide insights into how the house has evolved over the years.

Explore the various rooms and living spaces within the Boyles House. Many historic homes have preserved period-appropriate furnishings and decor, allowing visitors to experience the lifestyle of the past. Admire the architectural details, from ornate moldings to vintage fixtures, that contribute to the house's unique character.

Discover any artifacts, photographs, or documents on display that provide a deeper understanding of the Boyles House's history. Historical homes often house archives or exhibits that shed light on the local community, social customs of the time, and the evolution of the neighborhood.

Wander through the surrounding gardens or grounds, if applicable. The landscaping may have been designed with historical accuracy or adapted to modern tastes while preserving the overall ambiance of the property. Enjoy the serenity of the outdoor spaces and imagine the events that may have unfolded there.

Ask questions and engage with your tour guide to gain additional insights. Guides are typically well-versed in the history of the house and the broader historical context of the region. Take advantage of the opportunity to delve deeper into any aspects that pique your interest.

Capture the ambiance and architectural beauty of the Boyles House through photographs. Many historic homes encourage photography (following any guidelines set by the property), allowing you to create lasting memories of your visit and share the charm of the residence with others.

Consider the role of the Boyles House in the community and how it reflects the history of Birmingham. Historic homes often serve as windows into the past, offering a tangible connection to the people and events that shaped the local area.

Express gratitude to your guide and the staff responsible for preserving and sharing the history of the Boyles House. Consider leaving feedback or supporting any preservation efforts to ensure that future generations can continue to enjoy and learn from this piece of history.

Reflect on the experience as you leave the Boyles House. Whether you're a history enthusiast, an architecture buff, or someone intrigued by the stories embedded in historic homes, the tour provides a captivating journey into the past and a deeper appreciation for Birmingham's cultural heritage.

# 93. Attend the Market at Pepper Place.

Start your day at the Market at Pepper Place by strolling through the lively outdoor market. The atmosphere is likely bustling with activity, with vendors setting up colorful stalls and visitors perusing the diverse offerings.

Explore the fresh produce section, where local farmers display a bounty of fruits, vegetables, and other seasonal goods. Engage with the farmers, learn about their sustainable practices, and select some fresh ingredients to take home.

Browse the artisanal goods section, where local craftsmen and artists showcase their creations. From handmade jewelry to unique home decor items, this area provides an opportunity to discover one-of-a-kind pieces created by Birmingham's talented artisans.

Indulge your taste buds by sampling the diverse array of food options. Food vendors and local eateries may offer a tempting selection of ready-to-eat treats, from gourmet snacks to international cuisine. Consider trying something new or savoring a favorite dish.

Connect with the community as you meander through the market. Strike up conversations with vendors, fellow shoppers, and local artisans. The Market at Pepper Place is not just a place to shop; it's a social hub where you can experience the warmth and friendliness of the local community.

Enjoy live music or entertainment if it's featured at the market. Many farmers' markets incorporate musical performances or other entertainment to enhance the overall experience. Find a spot to relax, listen to the tunes, and soak in the lively ambiance.

Attend any workshops or demonstrations that may be taking place. The market often hosts educational sessions on topics such as cooking, gardening, or sustainable living. These activities provide valuable insights and add an interactive element to your visit.

Sip on a refreshing beverage as you explore. Whether it's freshly brewed coffee, a fruit smoothie, or a cold-pressed juice, there's likely a variety of beverages to keep you energized and hydrated throughout your market journey.

Capture the vibrant scenes and unique finds through photographs. Documenting your visit allows you to share the market experience with friends and family, and it's a great way to remember the local products and artisans you discovered.

Support local businesses by making purchases from the vendors. Whether you're buying fresh produce, handmade crafts, or delicious treats, your support contributes to the sustainability of local businesses and the overall vitality of the community.

Reflect on the Market at Pepper Place experience as you leave. Whether you came for the fresh produce, artisanal goods, or the sense of community, the market provides a dynamic and engaging way to connect with Birmingham's local culture and celebrate the creativity of its residents.

# 94.Explore the historic Bethel Baptist Church.

Commence your exploration of the historic Bethel Baptist Church by arriving at its distinguished location in Birmingham. Take a moment to appreciate the architectural features of the church, which may reflect the era in which it was constructed.

Step inside the church, where you'll likely encounter an atmosphere steeped in history. Many historic churches, including Bethel Baptist, have preserved their sanctuaries and key areas to retain the authenticity of the period. Observe the architectural details, stained glass windows, and any original furnishings that contribute to the church's character.

Learn about the rich history of Bethel Baptist Church by engaging with informative displays or attending guided tours. Gain insights into the church's founding, its role in the local community, and its significance during the Civil Rights Movement. Bethel Baptist has historical ties to the Reverend Fred Shuttlesworth, a key figure in the fight against segregation.

Explore the areas of the church that played a crucial role in civil rights activities. Many historic churches served as meeting places, strategy centers, and sanctuaries during this pivotal time. Bethel Baptist Church, in particular, hosted meetings of the Alabama Christian Movement for Human Rights and was a target of violence due to its involvement in the civil rights struggle.

Visit the Fred L. Shuttlesworth Museum if available, as it may be housed within or near the church premises. This museum could offer a deeper dive into the life and contributions of Reverend Fred Shuttlesworth, providing context for Bethel Baptist Church's significance in the Civil Rights Movement.

Reflect in the church's sanctuary or designated contemplative spaces. Many visitors find a moment of reflection or prayer meaningful as they consider the historical events that unfolded within the walls of Bethel Baptist Church.

Attend any events or services that may be taking place at Bethel Baptist. Many historic churches continue to be active places of worship, and participating in a service can provide a more comprehensive understanding of the church's present-day role in the community.

Capture the experience through photography, respecting any guidelines set by the church. Documenting your visit allows you to share the historical and cultural significance of Bethel Baptist Church with others.

Express gratitude to any guides or staff members who may have provided insights during your exploration. Consider leaving feedback or contributing to the preservation efforts of this historically significant church.

Contemplate the impact of Bethel Baptist Church on the Civil Rights Movement and its ongoing legacy. Whether you're drawn to the historical significance, the architectural beauty, or the spiritual aspects of the church, Bethel Baptist stands as a symbol of resilience and the pursuit of justice in American history.

# 95.Attend the Birmingham Boat Show.

Embark on your journey to the Birmingham Boat Show by entering the event venue, where you'll likely be greeted by the sight of a diverse array of boats. From sleek yachts to versatile fishing boats, the show typically features watercraft of various sizes and types. Take a moment to appreciate the craftsmanship and design that goes into each vessel.

Explore the exhibition halls housing marine accessories, gadgets, and fishing gear. Many boat shows complement the boat displays with vendors showcasing the latest technology, safety equipment, and recreational accessories. Whether you're an avid boater or a marine enthusiast, there's likely something of interest for everyone.

Engage with knowledgeable representatives from boat dealerships and manufacturers. They can provide insights into the features and specifications of different boats, helping you make informed decisions if you're considering a purchase. Ask questions and take advantage of the opportunity to learn about the latest trends in the boating industry.

Participate in interactive demonstrations and workshops that may be offered during the show. These sessions can cover topics such as navigation techniques, safety procedures, or the latest advancements in marine technology. Enhance your boating knowledge and skills through hands-on experiences.

Marvel at the luxurious interiors of some of the larger boats and yachts on display. Boat shows often feature vessels with lavish cabins, state-of-the-art entertainment systems, and innovative design elements. Even if you're not in the market for a high-end yacht, exploring these displays can be a captivating experience.

Check out the outdoor exhibits featuring boats in their natural element—floating on the water. Boat shows may offer on-water displays, allowing you to step aboard and get a feel for the boats in a real-life setting. Experience the thrill of being on the water without leaving the exhibition grounds.

Attend any special events or presentations scheduled during the Birmingham Boat Show. From guest speakers to live entertainment, these activities add an extra layer of excitement to the event. Consult the show schedule to make sure you don't miss any highlights.

Connect with fellow boating enthusiasts and share experiences. Boat shows provide a social setting where you can meet like-minded individuals, swap stories, and perhaps even make plans for future boating adventures.

Capture the excitement of the Birmingham Boat Show through photographs. Documenting your favorite boats, accessories, and memorable moments allows you to share the experience with friends and family.

Consider any purchases or make note of products and boats that caught your eye. Many vendors offer special discounts or promotions during boat shows, providing an opportune moment to make acquisitions or plan for future purchases.

As you leave the Birmingham Boat Show, reflect on the wealth of information, inspiration, and connections you've gained. Whether you're a seasoned boater or someone with a newfound interest in marine activities, the boat show offers a comprehensive overview of the boating world and its ever-evolving offerings.

# 96.Take a hot air balloon ride over the city.

Your hot air balloon adventure begins as you arrive at the designated launch site, likely a scenic location with expansive views of Birmingham and its surroundings. Feel the anticipation build as the balloon crew prepares the vibrant and gracefully floating vessel for your journey.

Climb into the spacious and sturdy basket, where you'll join your fellow passengers and the experienced balloon pilot. As the burner roars to life, the balloon starts to rise, offering a gentle and smooth ascent into the sky. Watch the ground below gradually fade away as the balloon gracefully lifts off.

As you ascend, a sense of tranquility envelops you. The silence, interrupted only by the occasional burst of the burner, contrasts with the bustling city life below. Witness the cityscape transform into a miniature world, with iconic landmarks, neighborhoods, and natural features unfolding beneath you.

Gaze in awe at the patchwork of buildings, parks, and waterways that define Birmingham. The panoramic views stretch out in all directions, providing a unique and immersive experience that few get to witness.

The gentle drift of the balloon allows for unhurried observation. You might spot familiar landmarks like Vulcan Park, the downtown skyline, or the serpentine flow of the Cahaba River. The pilot's knowledge of the area adds a layer of insight, as they point out noteworthy sights and share stories about the city's history.

Capture the magic of the moment through photographs, as the changing light casts a warm glow over the city. The unique vantage point from the balloon basket provides countless opportunities for stunning shots, whether you're capturing the city at sunrise, daytime splendor, or the glow of sunset.

Experience the thrill of being suspended in the air, gently drifting with the wind. The sensation of weightlessness and the unobstructed views make the hot air balloon ride a truly memorable and serene adventure.

As the journey nears its conclusion, the balloon begins its descent. The pilot skillfully guides the balloon to a gentle landing, where the ground crew awaits to assist with the process. Touching down, you'll feel a sense of accomplishment and gratitude for the extraordinary experience.

Celebrate the completion of your hot air balloon ride with a traditional toast, a customary practice in ballooning. Share stories with your fellow passengers and the crew, reliving the highlights of your aerial adventure over Birmingham.

Reflect on the unique perspective gained from soaring high above the city. The hot air balloon ride not only provides a thrilling and picturesque experience but also fosters a deep appreciation for the beauty and complexity of Birmingham from a new and elevated viewpoint.

# 97. Attend the Birmingham RV Super Show.

Your adventure at the Birmingham RV Super Show begins as you enter the exhibition venue, where a vast array of RVs awaits your exploration. From compact trailers to luxurious motorhomes, the show features a diverse selection of vehicles catering to different travel preferences and lifestyles.

Wander through the aisles of the RV show, marveling at the innovative designs and features of the displayed vehicles. Knowledgeable representatives from various RV manufacturers and dealerships are on hand to provide information, answer questions, and offer insights into the unique features of each model.

Step inside the different RVs to get a feel for their layouts, amenities, and comfort levels. Whether you're interested in a cozy camper for solo adventures or a spacious motorhome for family vacations, the Birmingham RV Super Show provides an opportunity to explore a wide range of options and find the perfect fit for your travel needs.

Engage with vendors and exhibitors showcasing camping gear, outdoor accessories, and the latest innovations in RV technology. From awnings and grills to solar panels and high-tech gadgets, the show offers a comprehensive look at the tools and accessories that can enhance your RVing experience.

Attend seminars and workshops hosted by industry experts. The Birmingham RV Super Show often includes educational sessions covering topics such as RV maintenance, travel tips, and outdoor adventure planning. Take advantage of these opportunities to expand your knowledge and make the most of your RV lifestyle.

Explore the outdoor recreation area where you may find activities like rock climbing walls, zip lines, or even a camping setup to experience firsthand. These interactive elements add an extra layer of excitement to your RV show experience.

Connect with fellow RV enthusiasts, sharing stories and tips about your own travel experiences. The RV community is known for its camaraderie, and the Birmingham RV Super Show provides a friendly environment to meet like-minded individuals who share a passion for outdoor exploration.

Take advantage of exclusive show deals and promotions. Many RV dealers offer special pricing or incentives during the show, making it an opportune time to make a purchase or upgrade your current RV setup.

Capture the highlights of the Birmingham RV Super Show through photographs. Document your favorite RV models, innovative accessories, and memorable moments to share with friends and family or as a reference for future RV considerations.

As you leave the Birmingham RV Super Show, reflect on the wealth of information, inspiration, and new connections you've gained. Whether you're a seasoned RV enthusiast or a novice exploring the world of RV travel, the show offers a comprehensive and immersive experience that fuels your excitement for outdoor adventures on the road.

# 98.Explore the Cahaba River National Wildlife Refuge.

Begin your journey at the Cahaba River National Wildlife Refuge by entering the designated access points, where you'll likely find trailheads, informational kiosks, and signs highlighting the refuge's ecological significance. Before setting out, take a moment to familiarize yourself with any trail maps or guidelines provided.

Embark on a hike along the refuge's trails, which meander through diverse habitats, including bottomland hardwood forests, wetlands, and riparian areas. The trails offer a chance to witness the beauty of the Cahaba River ecosystem and its unique flora and fauna. Keep an eye out for native plants, wildflowers, and the potential sighting of resident and migratory birds.

Follow the trails leading to scenic overlooks of the Cahaba River, providing opportunities for birdwatching and taking in the picturesque views of the waterway. The Cahaba River is known for its biodiversity, including several rare and endangered species, making it a haven for wildlife enthusiasts and conservationists alike.

Consider bringing binoculars or a camera to capture the vibrant birdlife that inhabits the refuge. The Cahaba River is particularly renowned for its role as a habitat for the imperiled Cahaba lily, an aquatic flowering plant that blooms in spring and adds to the visual appeal of the landscape.

Explore the wetlands and marshy areas, observing the rich variety of aquatic plants and the potential for glimpses of amphibians, reptiles, and waterfowl. The refuge's commitment to preserving these habitats contributes to the overall health of the Cahaba River ecosystem.

Engage in wildlife observation from designated viewing areas or bird blinds strategically placed throughout the refuge. These locations provide a quiet and unobtrusive vantage point for observing the natural behaviors of the diverse wildlife that calls the Cahaba River National Wildlife Refuge home.

If water access is available and permitted, consider kayaking or canoeing along the Cahaba River. Paddling through the refuge provides a unique perspective, allowing you to experience the water's gentle flow and encounter additional aspects of the ecosystem.

Pack a picnic and enjoy a meal at designated picnic areas within the refuge. Take time to savor the tranquility of the surroundings and appreciate the efforts made to conserve this ecologically important area.

Respect the refuge's rules and guidelines to minimize your impact on the environment. Leave no trace, stay on designated trails, and adhere to any seasonal restrictions or special considerations in place for the protection of wildlife and their habitats.

As you conclude your exploration of the Cahaba River National Wildlife Refuge, take a moment to reflect on the natural wonders you've encountered and the importance of preserving such vital ecosystems. Whether you're a nature enthusiast, birdwatcher, or someone seeking a peaceful retreat, the refuge offers a haven for connecting with the beauty of the Cahaba River and its surrounding landscapes.

# 99. Attend the Birmingham Military Tattoo.

Prepare for a spectacular display of military precision and musical excellence as you attend the Birmingham Military Tattoo. The event is likely held in a prominent venue, with a grandstand set up for the audience to enjoy the performances.

As you take your seat, the atmosphere is filled with anticipation. The sound of military drums and brass instruments creates a sense of ceremonial grandeur, setting the tone for an evening of patriotic and stirring performances.

The event begins with a traditional military parade, featuring soldiers in immaculate uniforms marching in precise formations. The rhythmic beat of drums and the synchronized movements of the drill teams showcase the discipline and training of the military personnel.

The military bands take center stage, presenting a repertoire that encompasses a mix of patriotic tunes, traditional military marches, and perhaps contemporary selections. The power and precision of the music reverberate through the venue, creating a sense of pride and admiration for the skill of the musicians.

Ceremonial displays, such as the Changing of the Guard or other symbolic acts, may be incorporated into the program. These moments pay homage to military traditions and highlight the commitment of the armed forces to duty and honor.

Witness impressive solo performances, where talented musicians or drill performers showcase their individual skills. Whether it's a virtuoso playing the bagpipes or a soloist delivering a moving rendition of a military anthem, these moments add a personal touch to the overall spectacle.

The event may feature guest performers, such as vocalists or dancers, adding variety to the program and celebrating the diversity of talents within the military community.

The highlight of the Birmingham Military Tattoo could be a grand finale, where all participating military units join forces for a breathtaking and coordinated display. This might include intricate formations, flag ceremonies, and a final musical crescendo that leaves a lasting impression on the audience.

Throughout the tattoo, the audience is encouraged to participate, whether through applause, standing during national anthems, or joining in on familiar tunes. The sense of community and shared respect for the military personnel on display creates a bond among attendees.

As you leave the Birmingham Military Tattoo, the echoes of the powerful performances linger in your memory. The event serves as a tribute to the dedication and skill of the military, fostering a sense of appreciation for their service and highlighting the rich traditions that contribute to the nation's history and identity.

# 100. Take a pottery class at MakeBHM.

Your pottery adventure at MakeBHM begins as you enter the vibrant and inspiring creative space. The atmosphere is filled with the hum of creativity, and the studio is equipped with all the tools and materials you'll need for your pottery class.

Greet your instructor, who is likely a skilled and passionate potter eager to guide you through the process. They'll introduce you to the basics of working with clay, the pottery wheel, and the various techniques you'll be exploring during the class.

Don your apron and take a seat at the pottery wheel, where a lump of clay awaits your artistic touch. The instructor provides step-by-step demonstrations, showing you how to center the clay and shape it into the beginnings of your pottery masterpiece.

Feel the tactile nature of the clay beneath your fingers as you immerse yourself in the creative process. The wheel spins, responding to your movements, as you mold and sculpt the clay into a form that reflects your artistic vision. The instructor offers personalized guidance, ensuring you feel confident and supported throughout the experience.

Experiment with different techniques, such as coiling, pinching, or carving, to add texture and detail to your pottery piece. The studio's array of tools allows for creativity and individual expression, and you'll discover the joy of shaping a three-dimensional work of art with your hands.

As your pottery creation takes shape, revel in the therapeutic and meditative aspects of working with clay. The tactile sensation, coupled with the rhythmic motion of the pottery wheel, creates a unique and immersive experience that fosters both relaxation and artistic fulfillment.

Once your pottery piece is complete, it undergoes the drying and firing process, transforming it into a durable and finished work of art. While waiting for your creation to be ready, take the opportunity to connect with fellow class participants, sharing insights and celebrating the collective creativity in the studio.

Return to MakeBHM to glaze and finish your fired pottery piece, adding the final touches that bring your vision to life. The vibrant colors and glossy finish enhance the aesthetic appeal of your creation, making it truly unique and reflective of your artistic style.

Celebrate the completion of your pottery class with a sense of accomplishment and newfound skills in the art of pottery. Your finished piece serves as a tangible reminder of your creative journey at MakeBHM and the joy of bringing something beautiful into the world with your own hands.

Reflect on the experience as you leave the studio, considering the therapeutic benefits of working with clay and the sense of community fostered by the shared creative space at MakeBHM. Whether you're a beginner or an experienced potter, the pottery class at MakeBHM offers a memorable and enriching artistic adventure.

# 101.Attend the Birmingham Multicultural Festival.

Enter the festival grounds with a sense of anticipation as the air is filled with a medley of cultural music, vibrant colors, and the enticing aroma of diverse cuisines. The Birmingham Multicultural Festival is likely held in a central location, where stages, stalls, and interactive areas showcase the city's multicultural spirit.

Engage with the lively crowd as you explore the festival grounds. Each area represents different cultures through art, music, dance, and culinary delights. Stroll through vibrant market stalls featuring handcrafted goods, traditional clothing, and unique artifacts from around the world.

Visit the stages where performers from various cultural backgrounds showcase their talents. Enjoy the rhythmic beats of international music, marvel at traditional dance performances, and witness live demonstrations of cultural arts and crafts. The festival's diverse lineup reflects the inclusivity of Birmingham's community.

Savor the flavors of the world at the international food stalls scattered throughout the festival. From exotic spices to familiar comfort foods, the culinary offerings provide a gastronomic journey that mirrors the city's multicultural essence. Don't hesitate to try new dishes and engage in conversations with the chefs about the cultural significance of each delicacy.

Participate in interactive workshops and cultural activities designed to foster understanding and appreciation. Whether it's learning traditional dances, trying your hand at crafting, or engaging in language exchanges, the festival offers opportunities to connect with various cultures on a personal level.

Attend cultural exhibitions and displays that highlight the history, traditions, and contributions of different communities in Birmingham. Informative panels and storytelling sessions may provide insights into the multicultural fabric that defines the city.

Bring the family, as the Birmingham Multicultural Festival often includes a dedicated area for children with activities, games, and educational experiences. The festival aims to be inclusive and welcoming to attendees of all ages, fostering a sense of unity among generations.

Connect with community organizations and multicultural associations that may have booths or information hubs at the festival. Learn about ongoing initiatives, volunteer opportunities, and ways to get involved in promoting diversity and understanding within the city.

Capture the vibrant moments of the festival through photographs, documenting the colorful displays, expressive performances, and the joyful interactions among attendees. Share your experiences on social media to spread the message of cultural appreciation and unity.

As you bid farewell to the Birmingham Multicultural Festival, reflect on the beauty of the shared experiences, the connections made, and the celebration of diversity. The festival serves as a testament to the city's commitment to embracing and cherishing the myriad cultures that collectively contribute to the unique identity of Birmingham.

# 102.Explore the Vulcan Trail.

Embark on your adventure by entering the trailhead of the Vulcan Trail, likely situated near Vulcan Park. The trail is known for its well-maintained paths, making it accessible to hikers of various skill levels. Before you begin, take a moment to appreciate the surrounding greenery and the anticipation of the scenic views ahead.

As you ascend the trail, enjoy the serenity of the natural surroundings. The Vulcan Trail is designed to showcase the beauty of the Birmingham landscape, providing a peaceful retreat from the hustle and bustle of city life. The rustling of leaves and the occasional bird's song create a harmonious backdrop for your journey.

Ascend to higher elevations, and you'll be rewarded with panoramic views of Birmingham's skyline and the surrounding hills. The vantage points along the trail offer opportunities to capture stunning photographs, especially during sunrise or sunset when the city below is bathed in warm hues.

Encounter informative markers along the trail that may provide insights into the local flora, fauna, and geological features. These educational elements enhance the hiking experience, allowing you to deepen your understanding of the natural environment.

Pass through sections of lush vegetation, perhaps shaded by tall trees, creating a pleasant and cool atmosphere. The diversity of plant life along the Vulcan Trail adds to the overall charm of the hike, making it an immersive nature experience within the city limits.

Reach the high point of the trail, where you can marvel at the iconic Vulcan statue standing tall against the backdrop of the sky. The observation points offer a unique perspective of the city and its landmarks, providing an excellent opportunity for reflection and relaxation.

Consider extending your hike by connecting to other nearby trails, allowing for a more extensive exploration of the Birmingham area. Many trail systems interconnect, providing options for varying lengths and difficulty levels to suit your preferences.

Bring along a water bottle and snacks to stay refreshed during your hike. The Vulcan Trail is designed for a leisurely outdoor experience, and having essentials ensures you can fully enjoy the journey.

As you conclude your hike along the Vulcan Trail, take a moment to savor the sense of accomplishment and the rejuvenating effects of spending time in nature. Whether you're a solo hiker seeking solitude or exploring with friends and family, the Vulcan Trail offers a delightful escape into Birmingham's natural beauty.

# 103.Attend the Birmingham Big Art Show.

Assuming a fictional scenario where there is a "Birmingham Big Art Show," attending such an event would likely provide a captivating experience. Here's a fictional exploration of what you might encounter:

Enter the bustling venue hosting the Birmingham Big Art Show, where the air is infused with creativity, and a diverse array of artworks awaits your exploration. The event is likely to feature a wide range of artistic expressions, including paintings, sculptures, installations, and multimedia creations.

Stroll through the curated galleries and exhibition spaces, each showcasing the talents of local and international artists. Engage with the art on display, taking in the myriad colors, textures, and conceptual depths that define each piece. Whether you're a seasoned art enthusiast or a casual observer, the Birmingham Big Art Show caters to a variety of tastes and preferences.

Meet and interact with the artists themselves, gaining insights into their creative processes and the inspirations behind their works. The opportunity to connect with the creators adds a personal touch to the art-viewing experience and fosters a deeper appreciation for the stories embedded in each piece.

Experience live art demonstrations, where artists may be creating new works on-site. Witnessing the artistic process firsthand provides a unique perspective and allows you to engage with the artists as they bring their visions to life.

Attend art talks and panel discussions featuring experts and critics in the art world. These sessions offer intellectual insights into the various genres, techniques, and cultural influences shaping contemporary art, providing an educational component to your visit.

Explore outdoor installations and interactive art experiences that extend beyond traditional gallery spaces. The Birmingham Big Art Show may incorporate public art displays, performance art, or temporary installations that transform the cityscape into an immersive gallery.

Support local artists by perusing the art market or participating in auctions. This allows you to take home a piece of the Birmingham art scene while directly contributing to the thriving local creative community.

Immerse yourself in the vibrant atmosphere created by a diverse community of art enthusiasts. Engage in conversations with fellow attendees, share perspectives on the art, and perhaps make new connections with people who share your passion for creativity.

Capture the moments by taking photographs of your favorite artworks and installations. Documenting your experience allows you to revisit the event's highlights and share your discoveries with others.

As you exit the Birmingham Big Art Show, reflect on the inspiration gained, the new perspectives encountered, and the role of art in fostering cultural richness and community engagement. Whether you leave with a new piece for your collection or simply a broader appreciation for artistic expression, the art show becomes a memorable and enriching experience within the cultural landscape of Birmingham.

# 104.Take a scenic drive along Mount Laurel.

Begin your scenic drive in Mount Laurel, where the roads are likely lined with towering trees and lush greenery. The air is filled with the sweet fragrance of blooming flowers, creating a refreshing and inviting atmosphere.

As you navigate the winding roads, you'll be treated to panoramic views of the surrounding hills and valleys. Mount Laurel's topography provides varying elevations, offering scenic overlooks that showcase the natural beauty of the area.

Pass through quaint neighborhoods adorned with charming houses, each nestled into the landscape with its unique character. The architecture may range from traditional to modern, contributing to the diverse charm of Mount Laurel.

Take a leisurely pace to appreciate the small details along the route. You may encounter babbling brooks, peaceful meadows, or even wildlife that adds to the enchantment of the drive. Keep an eye out for designated pull-off areas where you can pause and immerse yourself in the tranquility of the surroundings.

Consider visiting any parks or recreational areas along the way. Mount Laurel is likely to have outdoor spaces that allow for a closer connection to nature, whether it's a serene lake, a well-maintained trail, or a charming picnic spot. These detours add an extra layer of enjoyment to your scenic drive.

During certain times of the year, the foliage along Mount Laurel's roads may burst into vibrant hues of red, orange, and yellow, creating a breathtaking autumnal display. If your drive coincides with the fall season, savor the beauty of the changing leaves.

Capture the scenic moments with your camera, documenting the captivating landscapes and unique features that make Mount Laurel a special destination. The photographs serve as lasting mementos of your tranquil journey.

If there are any local landmarks or points of interest, consider incorporating them into your route. Whether it's a historic site, a charming cafe, or an art gallery, these stops can enhance your overall experience and provide opportunities for exploration.

As your scenic drive along Mount Laurel nears its conclusion, take a moment to reflect on the tranquility and natural beauty you've encountered. Whether you embarked on the journey for relaxation, inspiration, or simply to enjoy the open road, Mount Laurel's scenic drive offers a peaceful escape into nature's embrace.

# 105.Attend a performance at the Terrific New Theatre.

As you step into the Terrific New Theatre, the cozy and intimate atmosphere immediately welcomes you. The venue's design fosters a sense of closeness between the audience and the stage, creating an immersive experience that brings the performances to life.

Greeted by the anticipation of the upcoming show, you find your way to your seat. The intimate seating arrangement ensures that every audience member has a clear view of the stage, creating an atmosphere of shared excitement.

The lights dim, signaling the beginning of the performance. The stage comes alive with the energy and creativity of the actors, transporting you into the world of the play. The Terrific New Theatre's commitment to diverse and compelling productions means you could be in for a night of drama, comedy, or perhaps a thought-provoking piece of contemporary theater.

Throughout the performance, you become engrossed in the storytelling and the dynamic performances of the actors. The close proximity to the stage allows you to catch every nuance, facial expression, and emotion, creating a more intimate connection with the characters and the narrative.

Experience the synergy between the talented cast and the creative direction of the production. The Terrific New Theatre is likely to feature a range of performances, from classic plays to contemporary works, showcasing the versatility and skill of the local theater community.

Engage with the post-show atmosphere as you join fellow audience members in discussing the performance. The intimate setting encourages a sense of community, and you may have the opportunity to meet the actors, directors, or other theater enthusiasts.

Consider exploring the lobby or any art displays the theater may host. The Terrific New Theatre often supports local artists, and their exhibitions can add an extra layer of cultural enrichment to your visit.

As you leave the Terrific New Theatre, reflect on the emotional journey and artistic experience you've just encountered. Whether you were moved to laughter, tears, or contemplation, the theater's intimate setting and diverse repertoire contribute to a memorable evening of live performance art.

Supporting local theaters like the Terrific New Theatre fosters a vibrant cultural scene in Birmingham, and your attendance contributes to the continued growth and success of the performing arts community. Whether you're a seasoned theatergoer or a first-time attendee, the Terrific New Theatre offers a welcoming space to enjoy the magic of live theater.

# 106.Explore the Arlington-West End neighborhood.

Begin your exploration of the Arlington-West End neighborhood by strolling through its tree-lined streets. The residential areas are likely characterized by a mix of architectural styles, from historic homes with characterful details to more modern structures, creating a visually interesting tapestry.

Visit the local parks and green spaces that contribute to the neighborhood's relaxed atmosphere. Enjoy a leisurely walk or find a peaceful spot to sit and take in the surroundings. Parks in the Arlington-West End area may offer opportunities for outdoor activities and community gatherings.

Explore the historic landmarks that dot the neighborhood. Whether it's a well-preserved historic home, a landmark church, or other significant sites, these points of interest provide insights into the area's cultural and architectural history.

Take note of any local businesses, shops, or cafes that contribute to the neighborhood's unique character. Arlington-West End may boast a range of small businesses, each adding its flavor to the community. Consider stopping by a local cafe for a cup of coffee or exploring a boutique for unique finds.

Engage with the local community by attending neighborhood events or activities. Arlington-West End may host community gatherings, markets, or festivals that provide opportunities to connect with residents and get a feel for the vibrant community spirit.

Visit any local art galleries or cultural centers that showcase the creative talents of the community. These spaces often reflect the artistic and cultural diversity of the neighborhood, contributing to its dynamic and inclusive atmosphere.

Explore the local dining scene by trying out restaurants that offer a variety of cuisines. Whether it's a cozy diner, a family-owned eatery, or a trendy culinary spot, the Arlington-West End neighborhood is likely to have dining options that cater to different tastes.

Discover the local schools and educational institutions that contribute to the neighborhood's sense of community. Parks, libraries, and schools often serve as hubs for activities and events, fostering a strong sense of connection among residents.

Consider taking a self-guided walking tour of the neighborhood to appreciate its unique character and architectural highlights. This allows you to immerse yourself in the everyday life of Arlington-West End and discover hidden gems along the way.

As you conclude your exploration, take a moment to appreciate the sense of community and the local charm that defines the Arlington-West End neighborhood. Whether you're a resident or a visitor, the area's distinctive character and welcoming atmosphere make it a delightful place to explore and connect with the vibrant community.

# 107.Attend the Birmingham Music Festival.

Assuming a fictional scenario where there is a "Birmingham Music Festival," attending such an event would likely offer a vibrant and diverse musical experience. Here's a fictional exploration of what you might encounter:

Enter the lively atmosphere of the Birmingham Music Festival, where the air is filled with a symphony of melodies and the energy of music enthusiasts. The festival is likely held in a central location, featuring multiple stages and a lineup that spans various genres, from rock and pop to jazz, blues, and electronic music.

Explore the different stages, each hosting performances from local and international artists. Whether you're a fan of established bands or eager to discover emerging talent, the Birmingham Music Festival provides a platform for a wide range of musical expressions.

Immerse yourself in the diverse sounds and rhythms as you move between stages, encountering a kaleidoscope of musical genres. From the upbeat vibes of outdoor stages to the intimate settings of indoor venues, the festival's variety ensures there's something for everyone.

Engage in the communal spirit of the festival by joining the enthusiastic crowd. Dance to the beats, sing along to your favorite songs, and connect with fellow music lovers who share your passion for live performances.

Discover the food and beverage options scattered throughout the festival grounds. Whether it's a food truck offering local delicacies or a refreshing beverage station, the culinary offerings complement the overall festive experience.

Take a moment to explore any interactive installations or art exhibits that may be part of the festival. Many music festivals incorporate visual arts and immersive experiences to enhance the overall atmosphere and engage attendees in multi-sensory enjoyment.

Attendees might have the opportunity to meet and greet some of the artists, adding a personal touch to the overall experience. Artist signings, Q&A sessions, or even workshops may be part of the festival's programming, allowing for a deeper connection between performers and their fans.

Capture the vibrant moments of the festival by taking photos and videos. Share your experiences on social media, connecting with a broader community of music enthusiasts and extending the festival's reach beyond its physical location.

As the sun sets and the stages come alive with colorful lights, relish the evening performances that create a magical ambiance. The Birmingham Music Festival is likely to offer a memorable and immersive musical journey that leaves you with a sense of fulfillment and a collection of cherished memories.

# 108.Take a day trip to the American Village in Montevallo.

Arrive at the American Village in Montevallo, greeted by the picturesque surroundings and the architectural charm reminiscent of early American history. The campus is likely designed to transport visitors back in time, creating an immersive experience.

Begin your journey with a visit to the National Veterans Shrine, a symbolic and solemn space honoring the sacrifices of American veterans. Explore the exhibits and displays that pay tribute to the nation's military history, fostering a deep appreciation for the bravery and service of those who have served.

Travel to Birmingham Alabama

Participate in a guided tour of Colonial Chapel, an architectural gem that echoes the style of early American churches. Learn about the religious and cultural influences that shaped communities during the colonial era, and appreciate the craftsmanship of the chapel's design.

Engage in interactive and educational programs at Constitution Hall, where the principles of American democracy and the drafting of the U.S. Constitution come to life. Experience the spirit of the Constitutional Convention through reenactments and exhibits, gaining insights into the founding ideals of the nation.

Take a leisurely stroll through Liberty Bell Garden, a tranquil space featuring gardens and pathways that provide a peaceful retreat. The landscaping and design reflect the aesthetics of early American gardens, offering a serene environment for reflection.

Attend a live historical reenactment or performance at the Colonial Courthouse. The American Village often hosts theatrical presentations that bring pivotal moments in American history to the forefront, making the past come alive through engaging storytelling and authentic costumes.

Visit the Oval Office replica, a detailed recreation of the President's workplace. Explore the symbolism embedded in the design and layout of the Oval Office, gaining a deeper understanding of the presidential role in American governance.

Partake in educational workshops or activities, especially if you're visiting with family or a group. The American Village frequently offers hands-on experiences that cater to different age groups, making history accessible and enjoyable for everyone.

Enjoy a picnic in Constitution Village, surrounded by the charming architecture and ambiance of a colonial-era village. The American Village provides an ideal setting for a leisurely lunch, allowing you to absorb the historical atmosphere.

Before concluding your day trip, visit the gift shop to find unique souvenirs and educational materials related to American history. Whether it's books, replicas, or keepsakes, the shop offers mementos to commemorate your visit to the American Village.

As you bid farewell to the American Village in Montevallo, reflect on the insights gained, the historical narratives explored, and the significance of preserving and celebrating America's rich cultural heritage. Whether you're a history enthusiast, a student, or a family seeking an educational outing, the American Village provides a memorable and immersive experience that connects visitors with the roots of the nation's history.

# 109.Explore the Brown-Marx Building.

Arrive at the Brown-Marx Building, an iconic structure that stands as a testament to Birmingham's architectural heritage. The building, likely situated in the heart of the city, is characterized by its distinctive design and historical significance.

Begin your exploration by marveling at the exterior of the Brown-Marx Building. Appreciate the architectural details that reflect the style of the early 20th century, with features that may include intricate masonry, decorative elements, and a sense of grandeur that speaks to the era's industrial prosperity.

Enter the building and explore its interior, imagining the bustling activity that once filled its halls during its heyday. The lobby may showcase elements of Art Deco or Beaux-Arts design, providing a glimpse into the sophistication and elegance of the period.

Ascend to the upper floors to enjoy panoramic views of Birmingham from the Brown-Marx Building's vantage point. Take note of the cityscape, observing how it has evolved over the years while appreciating the building's role in shaping the skyline.

If the Brown-Marx Building has been repurposed, explore any contemporary uses or businesses that now inhabit its spaces. Adaptive reuse projects often breathe new life into historic structures, blending the old with the new to serve modern needs while preserving the building's historical character.

Learn about the history of the Brown-Marx Building through informative displays, plaques, or guided tours. Many historic buildings provide insights into their past, detailing their construction, original purpose, and significant events that occurred within their walls.

Capture the beauty and architectural details of the Brown-Marx Building through photography. Documenting your visit allows you to share the experience with others and creates a personal memento of your exploration.

If there are any nearby historical sites or points of interest, consider incorporating them into your visit. Birmingham's urban landscape often features a mix of historic and contemporary landmarks, creating a rich tapestry of experiences within walking distance.

Reflect on the Brown-Marx Building's role in Birmingham's history and its significance as a cultural and architectural landmark. Consider how the building's story intersects with the broader narrative of the city's development, from its industrial roots to its present-day identity.

As you conclude your exploration of the Brown-Marx Building, you may leave with a deeper appreciation for the preservation of historic structures and their role in connecting us to the past. Whether you're an architecture enthusiast, a history buff, or someone seeking a unique urban adventure, the Brown-Marx Building offers a captivating journey through time and design in the heart of Birmingham.

# 110.Attend the Barber Vintage Festival.

Arrive at Barber Motorsports Park, the iconic venue for the Barber Vintage Festival. The air is charged with excitement as the rumble of engines and the distinct sounds of motorcycles fill the atmosphere, creating an immediate sense of camaraderie among fellow enthusiasts.

Explore the sprawling grounds of Barber Motorsports Park, where a diverse array of motorcycles is on display. The Vintage Motorcycle Show features rare and classic bikes, each with its unique story and meticulously preserved or restored to its former glory. Marvel at the craftsmanship and design of motorcycles spanning different eras.

Witness the thrilling action on the race track as vintage motorcycles roar to life during racing events. Whether it's the Barber Vintage Motorsports Museum's Vintage Motorcycle Race or other competitions, the skill and speed of the riders add an adrenaline-fueled dimension to the festival.

Participate in or watch the annual Barber Small Bore Race, where riders navigate the challenging course on smaller displacement bikes, showcasing their agility and racing prowess. The race fosters a lively and competitive spirit, creating a memorable spectacle for spectators.

Engage with motorcycle enthusiasts and experts at seminars and workshops held during the festival. Topics may range from restoration techniques and maintenance tips to discussions on the cultural impact of motorcycles. These sessions provide valuable insights and foster a sense of community among attendees.

Peruse the Barber Vintage Motorsports Museum, home to one of the world's most extensive collections of vintage and modern motorcycles. The museum's exhibits offer a comprehensive journey through the history of motorcycling, featuring iconic models and rare gems that span decades.

Explore the vendor and exhibitor area, where motorcycle-related businesses, artisans, and collectors showcase their products and services. This marketplace is an opportunity to discover unique gear, accessories, and memorabilia, making it a haven for motorcycle enthusiasts looking to enhance their riding experience.

Immerse yourself in the vibrant social scene of the festival, where enthusiasts gather to share stories, swap tips, and revel in their shared passion for motorcycles. The festival's atmosphere fosters a sense of camaraderie, creating lasting connections among attendees.

Attend the Barber Vintage Festival Nighttime Paddock Party, where the festivities continue after the sun sets. Live music, food trucks, and a lively atmosphere transform the paddock into a vibrant social hub, allowing attendees to unwind and celebrate their shared love for motorcycles.

Capture the memorable moments of the Barber Vintage Festival through photographs and videos. Documenting the unique bikes, races, and the overall atmosphere allows you to relive the experience and share it with fellow motorcycle enthusiasts.

Travel to Birmingham Alabama

As you conclude your time at the Barber Vintage Festival, you may leave with a deeper appreciation for the culture, history, and community surrounding motorcycles. Whether you're a seasoned rider, a vintage bike enthusiast, or someone new to the world of motorcycles, the festival offers an immersive and exhilarating celebration of two-wheeled passion at Barber Motorsports Park.

# Conclusion

Birmingham, Alabama, has a rich and multifaceted history that has shaped its identity and contributed to its evolution as a prominent Southern city. From its humble beginnings as an industrial hub fueled by mining and manufacturing to its pivotal role in the Civil Rights Movement, Birmingham has undergone significant transformations.

The city's founding in the aftermath of the Civil War marked the beginning of its industrial ascent, with the discovery of valuable iron and coal deposits propelling it into a leading industrial center. This rapid growth brought about prosperity but also underscored social and economic disparities, laying the groundwork for Birmingham's complex societal fabric.

The mid-20th century saw Birmingham at the forefront of the Civil Rights Movement, earning a place in history for both its staunch resistance to desegregation and the determined activism of its African American community. The events such as the Birmingham Campaign and the 16th Street Baptist Church bombing left an indelible mark, contributing to the national discourse on civil rights and racial justice.

As the city moved into the latter half of the 20th century, economic diversification became a priority, steering Birmingham away from its heavy reliance on the iron and steel industries. Efforts to revitalize downtown, coupled with cultural and educational initiatives, have transformed Birmingham into a dynamic urban center with a growing emphasis on technology, healthcare, and finance.

While contending with historical challenges, Birmingham continues to forge ahead, embracing its cultural heritage and fostering a sense of community resilience. The city's commitment to preserving its historical landmarks, such as the Civil Rights District and the Sloss Furnaces, reflects a dedication to honoring its past while embracing a progressive vision for the future.

In the 21st century, Birmingham stands as a city in transition, balancing its industrial legacy with a forward-looking approach to economic development and cultural enrichment. The diverse array of neighborhoods, vibrant culinary scene, and ongoing efforts to promote inclusivity contribute to Birmingham's dynamic character, making it a city with a compelling history and a promising future.

Travel to Birmingham Alabama

If you enjoyed, please leave a 5-star Amazon Review

To get a free list of people who knows publishing top places to travel all around the world, click this link
https://bit.ly/peoplewhoknowtravel

## References

Rcsprinter123, CC BY-SA 3.0 <https://creativecommons.org/licenses/by-sa/3.0>, via Wikimedia Commons
https://pixabay.com/photos/macarons-raspberries-pastries-2548827/

Made in the USA
Coppell, TX
11 October 2025

61141003R00098